Jenny 'n' Dad

THE LOVE STORY OF
A VERY YOUNG DAUGHTER
AND A VERY OLD DAD

GORDON BAXTER

SUMMIT BOOKS
NEW YORK

Published by SUMMIT BOOKS
A Division of Simon & Schuster, Inc.
Simon & Schuster Building
1230 Avenue of the Americas
New York, New York 10020
SUMMIT BOOKS and colophon are trademarks of
Simon & Schuster, Inc.
Designed by Eve Metz
Manufactured in the United States of America

1 3 5 7 9 10 8 6 4 2

Library of Congress Cataloging in Publication Data

Baxter, Gordon, date.
Jenny 'n' dad.

1. Baxter, Jenny Tittle, 1977–   . 2. Daughters—
Biography.   3. Fathers and daughters.   I. Title.
II. Title: Jenny 'n' dad.
HQ755.85.B385B39   1985   306.8'742'0924   85-2850

ISBN: 0-671-46954-1

TO DIANE

Contents

8   *Contents*

CHAPTER 1

Jenny

Sometimes Jenny and I go out and strut the mall at the shop-ping center as couples do in the evenings in little Texas towns. Holding hands, in easy talk, we pass along before the shop windows. We are people-watching, and feeling people watching us. We have a very special love, one that already feels the faint rush of time. The love of a very old daddy and a very young daughter. I am more than a half century older than Jenny.

Jenny says "Hi" to strangers as we stroll by them. They say "Hi" back and stop to talk. Many of them know us because I have been a newspaper writer and in radio and TV here all my life and I can't help but talk about Jenny.

But to some we are strangers. They see the resemblance between us. Jenny's face tends to the beauty of her mother's, but she has my strawberry-blond complexion and coloration. "She's beautiful," they say. "Your granddaughter?"

By my first family I have granddaughters older than Jenny. I curb the wild impulse to grab hands with Jenny and dance a ring around them, shouting, "No, you old coot, she's my DAUGHTER!" But Jenny and I are making some effort to curb where we do our wild dancing and shouting. So we stand very still, holding in the laughter, and I look at Jenny, her cue to say, "No, he is my father." Then we must stand and make a little polite talk, their eyes going over my old face and her fresh one while their minds try to figure out how this happened.

It's very simple, happens all the time. An old marriage of twenty-five or thirty years comes to a stop, opens up, the man steps out of it and marries a younger woman, and soon he is back in the baby business again. And with grown children of his own. A group I lovingly call "the first litter."

But Jenny is growing so fast. At four she was still chunky, a baby, I could carry her like a ball. At five, just a few minutes later it seemed, she was gazelle-legged. She dangled when I lifted her, and needed a lot less lifting. "Look, Dad, I can reach the light switches now."

Outside the mall we walked together in the long light toward the car. Long shadow, short shadow. "Jenny, you are my shadow, my constant companion." She laughed, pranced, made her shadow clown a little. "Daddy, I can beat you to the car."

At five I let her win. At six she was winning and she knew it.

While other men my age are carefully bagging leaves, my child and I are still finding first clover blossoms. Instead of turning to my memories, I am still answering her firsts of discovery. "Daddy, who makes clover?"

"OK, then who is God?"

"Then who made God?"

Sitting in fresh clover with a hand full of tiny yellow blossoms, Jenny and I contemplate the face of God. Like her mother's, Jenny's eyes tell you everything. Big and blue, in her headlong rush to know it all, to see it all. Like a fine camera, she's been storing images since she first saw the light.

Yes, I am rejoicing at being the first man in her life. Yes, I am aware that what we share will prepare her for success and happiness with the man I will someday give her away to. And, yes, I hear the distant bell tolling sometimes, knowing I will probably never see her as a woman of thirty.

For now, all this is my secret. Jenny the child has no idea of the pesky business of aging or dying. She just rejoices at each day, total love or total outrage, then coming close to say, "Daddy. I love you."

In my long lifetime I thought I had known every kind of love there is to know. But nothing could have prepared me for this. Nor would I have believed you had you tried to come and tell me of this very easy, very special love between a very old daddy and a very young daughter. No way could I have known that a child could mean so much to me so late in life.

CHAPTER 2

Diane

The special bonding between Jenny and me grew from the fullness of Diane's love. Even before Jenny was conceived, that special love began with who Diane is.

She graduated from high school as one of the least-known girls in her class. Diane was shy. As often happens among brighter students, Diane thought there might be something wrong with her.

Her beauty attracted boys, who were than confounded as to what to do with her on a date. When she was parked with one athlete he finally croaked, "Well what *do* you wanna do? You wanna run a foot race?" Diane said yes, they ran a foot race, and of course that one never called her back either.

Diane went to college. It was expected of her. She enrolled at little east-Texas colleges, first one, then another, making high grades, dropping out. Her unnamed discontent grew.

"So I decided to go fly the airlines," she said of herself. "There is no way to be shy as the stewardess, cooped up in an airliner cabin with forty strange men."

I met her just as she began to fly Braniff. We kept up a cryptic correspondence for about ten years. After my own marriage had ended I made a date to see her at her home in Dallas. Chickened out, then made another date and kept it. I decided she was the most beautiful woman I had ever met, wondered what she saw in me.

All I kept from my first marriage was my woods wilderness cabin, a rustic place that had become my home. The cabin fronted on a white sandbar of Village Creek about twenty miles north of my former home in Beaumont. Isolated, a quarter mile from the nearest neighbor, I loved the place. I had designed it and had taken three years to build it with the help of my first family and my friends. Most people would never live there, preferring a more snake- and spider-free home in town.

Diane came with me to visit the cabin and the creek. She instantly understood and shared my feelings about the place. The resident snake peeked out at Diane, who did not run or scream. "His name is Snavely, and he's friendly in a confused sort of a way," I explained.

Diane accepted Snavely and all the other creatures of the forest accepted Diane. We were married there on the broad, open-front, rockingchair gallery under low December skies. There was the cry of Canadian geese passing, which I took to be an omen of some kind.

We had brought all of Diane's things down from Dallas. She had a few cardboard boxes full of her clothes; the rest of that two-ton rented truck was full of her books. That was the real omen.

Her family was there, and mine. Hers came dressed in their Sunday best, mine looked as though they had flown in with the geese.

My only brother, Tom the Priest, read the words from his Episcopalian book. We knelt on the boards, our people stood in a circle around us. A caption for the wedding picture would have been hard to write had you not known us, for the groom and his mother-in-law looked to be about the same age and the bride and her stepdaughters did, too.

Afterward, inside the big warm central room of the cabin there was laughter and hugging and Diane and I sipped the wedding wine from new glasses, then flung the glasses to shatter against the wall.

Folks jumped. Some thought the fight had started already.

Overheard between two of my kids: "What are you going to give Dad and Diane?"

"Oh, about six weeks."

At first I worried about our nearly twenty-year age difference. I needn't have, for I know now that I will never be as old as Diane.

The real danger, the hidden shoal that lay ahead of us, was that our concepts of men and women came from different centuries. Diane is a self-sufficient twentieth-century woman who had lived by her own means all of her adult life. My concept of the roles of men and women was right out of the nineteenth century, and I couldn't see a thing wrong with that.

My old Daddy taught me that it is the man's place to make the living, and the woman's to make the living worthwhile. That the man was the good and faithful hunter, brought meat to the cave door. That the man was responsible, and along with the responsibility went his authority.

This father-to-son wisdom had served him well, and his father before that, and his father's father, and all the rest of them, all the way back to Scotland, all the way back to the cave.

The cave-man concept of man's work and woman's work that had served my ancestors well was laughable to Diane. "Just try thinking of me as a fellow human," she would say. "Think of me as your friend."

I tried. I opened up my work to her, for head-to-head talk about it, and was surprised to find that her keen mind and insightful reading began to improve both my writing and the broadcasting. "You married her for the wrong reasons," I mumbled to myself.

As Diane shared some of my role, I shared some of hers. Once when my kids came to visit and found me doing the dishes they took Diane aside to whisper. "We can't believe what you have done for the Ole Man. In all our lives we never saw him at the sink in an apron—or as contented and happy-looking."

In those first years Diane and I had to work at it—"allowing" for each other, we called it. But I was not ready for it when one solemn night she said, "I want our baby."

I had been through all that as a young man. Done my share and then some. With an unforgettably poor choice of words I said to her, "What do you want to do, mess up our playhouse?"

Green eyes ablaze, Diane sat straight up in bed, covers pulled up to her chin, and assured me that we were not "playing house!"

"You had your children, you saw them growing up. Would you deny me that? Deny me my womanhood?"

In past lovemaking I had heard Diane cry out, "Oh, I want your baby!" This I mistook as only a woman in the fullness of her passion.

And once before in one of our "get acquainted" talks—of who we were, what we did—she had told me of starting the tedious procedure of applying as a single parent to the adoption agencies in Dallas. I had never put all this together in my mind as a serious reading of what was, and had been, going on in her heart.

Now I looked into her eyes, her face, and realized again the foolishness of not listening very well. Of sometimes discounting her. Jenny was born in the fourth year of our marriage, on August 26, 1977.

CHAPTER 3

The Bonding

We lost the first one, a little boy child. On rainy nights when spirits howled up under the eaves and the trees huddled and swayed around the cabin, Diane in her grief would recall that scene in the emergency room and bite her lip, and tears would stream down her cheeks.

And she carried precariously with this one. Lying on the long couch, feet up on pillows, sensing the delicate clinging to life within her. She grew pale, until her gentle and understanding doctor told her to get on her feet, go on about her life. "You will either carry or you won't."

She bought and read a new maternity book for every week she was pregnant, and she wanted me to read them, too. I did, noticing that nobody has written anything for expectant fathers. She was proud of her new rounding. Stood before the mirror, glowing with inner light, loving the child within her. For the love of Diane I began to love our baby.

And then one peaceful and still night, as she lay on that same long couch, there was a shout. *"Life!* I felt life. Come here!" I was already up, startled to my feet. There was nothing that I could yet feel there in the warm crowding of curves, but in her eyes I could know at least something of the flutter, the quickening, she had felt beneath her heart. For days after that she moved in a dreamlike way, hugging and crooning to herself.

The pace quickened. She went out and found her sisters, she joined things. Lamaze, LaLeche, LaBooks, LaWitch doctors. I was dragged along, LeHusband, wondering how they did it back when they used to just circle the wagons and the women went off behind the bushes and squatted and took care of their business.

"They lost a lot of babies, that's how they did it!" snapped Diane. "And they lost a lot of mammas too. Little shallow graves in the prairie marked your westward trail, O mighty man!"

So I kept a civil tongue in my head and went along to baby-having classes. Stood there dumb as an ox, wondering what the other dumb-ox husbands were thinking as our wives lay in rotund rows, arms waving aloft like tall-stemmed tulips seeking the sun, their scented breaths filling the air as the stern drill matron counted out the cadences. And we practiced faithfully at home too, I wondering what help any of this would be. But we got good at it. At Lamaze.

At the fearful old age of thirty-six Diane insisted on all of the precautionary test procedures. I went along to the hospital thinking, What do you expect of an over-age, overread, emancipated educated woman calving for the first time?

But in the stark silence of the sonogram room when I first heard the light running footsteps of our baby's pitty-pat heart entwined with the steady bass-drum beat of her mother's, my heart was caught up in this, too.

The woman doctor, moving her sound scribe over Diane's belly, was talking to herself. "Rolled over again, didn't you? Quick little thing you are. Steady . . . right there. Oh, what a strong little heart. Listen to that good little heart!"

They were snapping pictures too, of the sound image, computer enhanced and displayed on a video screen. I was crowding over and craning to see. Our child, photographed but not yet born, seemed to be sitting at rest, knees drawn up to chin, arms clasping her knees. All the delicate tracery of fine bones, ample skull and searching eyes, at rest. Me, I'm leaning over waving into the window. "Hi, it's me, Dad . . ."

Little Monk, still huddled in there, yet in touch with all the mysteries of the world, before and after, borning and dying, and soon to come rejoicing out of there.

They were snapping Polaroid pictures, the doctor was scanning them quickly, satisfied, dropping them on the floor. Would you believe I left there without grabbing up at least one of them? I called back later, but they don't keep them if there's no problem. Oh, Jenny, what a picture I would have had to show the young men who come acalling. "And this is Jenny before she was born."

"Oh-h, Daddee-e."

The doctor's voice broke into this conversation between me and Jenny. She was talking to Diane, telling her all the good things, while the twin heartbeat patterns would fade, then rise, join and entwine, the amplified sound filling the room. I felt I should be kneeling down before God to be in the portals of a cathedral such as this.

The only birthing sounds I had heard before was when young husbands were kept locked out in the hospital corridors and the occasional muffled scream came to them through thick wooden doors. And sometimes a nun would come rustling by in starched whites and give me a glare. "See what you have done?" she seemed to say. I would stand there in the hallway with all the other tobacco-reeking men, each as guilty and worthless as I. "Woman's work." My dad.

All the tests showed a normal and healthy mother and child. Our baby got a better grip on her mommy, the last months went proudly and without fear.

And when Jenny came into this world I was in there, in the sweat of the labor, touching Diane, repeating the long-drilled Lamaze techniques, which seemed to be working.

"OK, Diane, pattern breathing now. You got only ten more seconds of this, then you can rest."

They call it "husband-coached childbirth." They should better call it "husband-assisted." There were times when Diane glared at me with bared teeth and I knew I was coaching nothing. Once in the hours between midnight and dawn when the room was crowded with nurses and doctors leaning over Diane and tubes and devices running here and there, she cried out, "Some of you get out of here! Give me room. Give me some air!" I was the one who went out—into the parking lot, where I sat down on a concrete curb and cried a little.

The clock hands dragged on into her tenth and eleventh hours of labor through a molasses of pain. "It's crowning," I would say to her. "Push," said the doctor. Diane drew up her knees and pushed with more human courage than I had ever stood beside. She would look at me, fingernails digging into my hand. All she could see was my face, hopeless in love and despair. Don't ever talk to me again about manly courage and endurance of pain.

She looked up at me with a trace of her old game humor around her lips. "If my hips had been two inches wider we'd be home by now," she said.

"If your hips had been two inches wider you'd never have gotten here in the first place," I replied in our tradition.

She closed her eyes again and whispered, "You dirty dog. I'll never let you forget that." Then she opened her eyes and smiled again.

She had been in labor twelve hours and I was surprised to see it was my hands that were trembling.

"High forceps," said the doctor. "Take her to the other room."

Diane squeezed my hand for mutual comfort. I was remembering my cavalier ideas of childbirth. Just circle the wagons, let 'em off behind the bushes. Had we been coming to Texas a hundred years ago it would have been I who dug one more lonely grave beside the westward trail.

Diane's continued courage was astonishing to me. She never cried out, she asked for a mirror to be placed so that she could watch. I will never forget the skilled manner in which that doctor manipulated those tongs against soft flesh. How their steel sometimes rang out like tire irons in a lonely garage at midnight. My job was to hold Diane's shoulders firmly against the pulling force from the doctor. I was taking courage from this woman between us.

The doctor raised his sweating hand. "I'm not subjecting

this child to any more trauma," he said, almost to himself. "Prepare C section."

Oh my God, I thought. My eyes met Diane's. Her lips formed "OK." The rest of it was swiftly done. As they rolled her between those double doors into surgery she waved a wan hand, as if she were only going through a garden gate.

I sat awhile in the waiting room, then had to pace. Everything that was going on in my mind was awful. I could not shut off my imagination. The cut across her taut roundness. Would he use the modern Bikini cut, low and horizontal? Oh you chauvinistic ass. She never wears a Bikini anyhow.

I paced and wrestled my demons. I lit my pipe, calmly observing the shaking of the match flame. The tobacco was foul to my nostrils. Time had groaned to a stop. I hung slowly by a thin umbilical cord, turning in the wind. Oh Diane, my Diane, don't let them hurt you. The belly I had blown my softest breath across.

Half the surgery-room door banged open, a little grinning nurse with hair matted to her forehead and her green mask down around her neck popped out the door. "It's a girl! A big one, Mr. Baxter. They are both fine." Then she was gone, and the closing door went *ps-sshht*. So did I. The breath I had been holding gone out of me. I settled into one of those rump-sprung waiting-room chairs. I wanted to laugh, but it was coming out as tears.

They rolled Jenny out in one of those little carts with the clear plastic dome. I knew she was Jenny. We had already decided if she was a girl we would call her Jenny. We were the only ones who didn't know she would be a girl. We had asked the testing people to make a note on our records that we were not to be told. Nobody had told us, although there had been a lot of teasing questions about whether we wanted a boy or a girl. Diane and I were both old-fashioned about this. If the Lord wanted you to know you were going to have a little girl, He would put pink bootees by your door.

A girl! I really was hoping for a girl, and couldn't tell you why. Now I was looking down at our Jenny in her cart. No little stranger this; I felt as if I already knew her. There she lay, all brand-new and pink, a thick mop of red hair crowning her fine head, dark-blue eyes squinting against the harsh light. She was waving and smiling up at me as if she had just set her suitcase down. I said, "Hiya, Jenny."

"Hi, Dad."

Then they trundled her off to the wash rack, or wherever they are in such a hurry to go with newborns. My little nurse friend popped out again and assured me Diane was OK, but they would be a little more time with her. I bet they would. I tried not to even think of them in there stitching her slippery mainsail back together again.

I looked around, and Cliff, an old friend and the family GP, was standing there, smiling. He had come out of nowhere and sat down to talk. After a time I realized he was doing some much-needed husband-sitting.

And then they brought me my Diane. She was worrying about how her hair looked, so I knew she was all right. Diane is like a cat: if she is not preening her fine shiny coat, then you know she is really very sick.

We went down the corridors to the room that would be our family home for a while. Diane was lifted into the bed. She settled herself down, risked all those stitches leaning over to rummage through the bedside drawer to find her hairbrush, and gave herself a few strokes. "How do I look?" she asked.

She looked as if she had just won the National Marathon. I gave her what little hugging one can do across a hospital bed and we waited for Jenny to come home.

At last there was a great stirring outside and we were given hospital greens and masks to wear. I watched Diane's face as Jenny was first handed into her waiting arms. Not just arms filled, but a life fulfilled. Diane held the hours-old Jenny to her breasts. "I can't believe this. Oh, I just can't believe this."

A few moments later, in this unforgettably poignant scene of mother and daughter, Daddy's song was born.

Jenny stiffened. She arched her strong little back and raised her voice in what was to be our introduction to her suffering with colic. Jenny began to howl and squirm. On some crazy impulse I reached for our daughter, and Diane handed Jenny to me. Never before would I have thought there was something I could do in this business of mother and child. I cradled Jenny firmly, raised one foot to stomp mightily, and began to sing and dance an old raucus hillbilly tune, "The Wabash Cannonball."

The hospital people drew back. Diane pretended she never knew me. Jenny stared up at me, wide-eyed. Then I swear she grinned at me. She gave a little sigh, relaxed and burrowed into my chest. We danced around, sang a few more verses, then in utter triumph I handed the calm and sleeping baby back to her mother. Daddy's song.

Colic was to become a worsening problem in the months ahead. A little hospital tragedy was about to face us now.

The doctor had told Diane it was almost a certainty that she would develop some infection from the complicated birth. As forecast, the infection manifested itself in Diane on the second day. Jenny was taken from her mother's breast.

In order to protect all the newborns in maternity, Diane was moved out and placed in the surgical recovery wing of the hospital. The wound of seeing her baby being carried away cut far deeper into Diane than the surgeon's knife had. Her face was a mask of controlled grief. And because Diane had the extra misfortune of being allergic to penicillin, a quick cure was ruled out. She was put on long-term antibiotics instead. There was never any danger or doubt about Diane's slow recovery; her agony was full breasts and empty arms. A lifetime of waiting to hold her own baby, then after two days Jenny was gone.

"She probably doesn't even know she has a mother. Oh, Gordon, please go stand by the nursery window and watch. Tell me everything she does. Tell me how she moves her hands. Can she turn her head from side to side? Does she still have the thick mane of red hair, or was that just a part of her birthday suit? Go watch for me, Gordon. Tell me everything. . . ."

I became the phantom of the hospital halls. The women of the nursery came to know my face. They knew the story too. There are no secrets in hospitals. I would come back after they pulled the curtain closed and tell Diane that Jenny had become the darling of the nursery. That she was actually in the arms of one of those big matrons in a rocking chair. That she was being snuggled and held and rocked and crooned to.

Diane would listen to me with empty eyes. Then wordlessly she would hold her swollen breasts and rock and croon to herself. The gods themselves could not have devised a more exquisite torture for my wife.

The doctor was compassionate. After ten days he reached the decision that, regardless of the risks, Diane and Jenny would be better off at home together. But even then the rules were carefully applied. One nurse saw a weakened Diane down the corridor and out the front door, another carried Jenny. Only outside in the driveway, outside the hospital's territorial waters, did they hand the baby back to her mother.

I don't think I have ever driven the familiar roads out to our place in the woods more carefully. I didn't want to bounce anybody. Diane had her head bent to Jenny in her arms. The baby was playing with the curtain of Diane's hair that enclosed their private world. They were talking only to each other.

At the cabin I asked Diane if I could do the Alex Haley scene at the creek and would she take a picture of us? She smiled up at me, nodded. I crossed the pure-white sandbar in front of the cabin, waded out into the clear shallows of Village Creek and there held Jenny up to God. "Your name is Jenny Tittle Baxter. Behold God, the only thing greater than yourself!" Then I carried Jenny up the wide gracious stairway and into our home.

Diane's mother was waiting for us. She took over and I was thankful. "You've done enough walking, Diane. Get into bed, I'll take care of things." And she did, putting the antique wooden cradle that had held Diane as a baby up beside Diane's bed.

Now the life had come back into Diane's face. "Look how

strong she is. Look how she can already hold up her head."
We all looked. Jenny held up her head and had a look for
herself. There was soft laughter in the house again.

The wise eyes of Grandma Sally missed nothing. She noticed that Diane was having trouble nursing, but said nothing.
She saw Jenny suddenly tighten with pain after the first few
hours home and laid an experienced hand on the baby's ach-
ing tummy. "Colic," she confirmed. She and Diane asked
each other whether it might be the formula we had brought
home from the hospital and were trying to bottle-feed Jenny.
And they talked about colic. How long would it last? What
was causing it? What to do next? A thoroughly professional
conversation. Sally had raised four of her own, and her first
granddaughter, Debbie, had been born ahead of Jenny.

I stood back from it. They reminded me of race car me-
chanics at the Indy 500. No place in these pits for an amateur.
Then Diane said, "Watch this." And handed Jenny to me.

I did Daddy's song, loud and with all the stomping. Sally's
eyes widened as Jenny relaxed and went to sleep. She and
Diane agreed it was probably self-defense.

Sally could stay only that day, went home to Dallas, partly
I think to let the three of us be alone. We hadn't been yet.

We enjoyed the peace of long silences. There was no need
to make talk. We were asleep by dark with Jenny beside us,
but it was to be a short night. Jenny began her pattern of
never sleeping much more than two hours without waking up
with a cry and a bellyache.

After one longer-than-usual sleep we woke up to find that
Jenny had managed to swap ends in the cradle. She went to
sleep facing east, woke up facing west. Both delighted and
alarmed, we put the antique crib away. The slats were too
widely spaced for such a rumpus kid, pushing and shoving her
noggin wherever she could.

CHAPTER 4

Daddy's Song

Diane was tireless in getting up to check on the baby. She went to see why Jenny cried. Then she would get up to see why she was so quiet.

We had enough real troubles right under the roof without borrowing more. Diane's surgical recovery was being delayed by pure and simple weariness. I built a set of hand rails to aid her in pulling herself up from the bed. That helped. And at least it made me feel I was doing something. There was no getting between Diane and the call of her child.

She set her mind to her dual problems, Jenny's colic and her own inability to breast-feed. She suspected that they were related. She read me a chapter from one of her books about how interrupted nursing in the first two weeks can cause a cessation of flow. She called in the ladies of the local LeLeche society; they counseled, but Diane began experimenting with different formulas, hoping to find one that would give her baby an easy belly. I had no idea there were so many formulas available. She searched Houston, Dallas, spoke to at least three different doctors. She tried goat's milk, soybean and one that was described as a meat formula. Hungry Jenny went for all of it, and got the bellyache just the same.

Diane expanded on the idea of Daddy's song. She played music at feeding time, all sorts of music, classical to hillbilly. She tried leaving the vacuum cleaner running. We still got no more than two hours' sleep. One doctor suggested allergy testing. Another prescribed drops to put under the baby's tongue before feeding. Jenny was game about it all. And still had colic. She would wake up abruptly, her belly tight with the pain.

"What can I do? Oh, what can I do?" Diane would bury her face in her hands, her shoulders shaking with her silent crying.

But she seldom allowed herself such despair. Mostly Diane was hopeful and searching for some solution. She even talked to one doctor who asked her to put the telephone to Jenny's belly so he could listen to it. Such scenes were a game to Jenny, and her ready laughter when she was not hurting would become instant laughter and a game to us too.

Despite her chronic hurting belly, we were discovering, Jenny was a bon vivant, a delight.

I discovered that walking gave relief to Jenny. I would pick her up in the night, go down the front steps and out to the hard-packed sand at the edge of the creek and walk with her held close to my bare chest. The crescent of sandbar is about three hundred yards long. We would walk and I would sing, at the top of my voice, to hear my own echo coming back from the dark wall of the forest across the creek. For a while I would see Diane's head at the window watching us, then no more and I knew she had gratefully gone back to sleep.

Jenny and I would walk and sing on the sandbar in the moonlight's beauty or under the cold darkness of distant Polaris. When the night Sante Fe freight slowed and blew for the roads just before crossing the Village Creek trestle, I would sing to the echo of the train whistle through the mile or so of forest.

As autumn rains caused sister creek to rise up and cover her sandbar we would walk my winding patty-foot sandy road beneath overhanging dark trees. With only a narrow path of cold starlight to guide us in the fresh autumn night, I would hold Jenny's wrapping blanket close and sing some old Mississippi John Hurt song. ". . . Like a tree planted by the water, I shall not be moved."

Out there singing in those woods I could feel the nearness of God and my daughter soaking right through to my soul. At least I think that's what was soaking through. I sang her all the verses of "Rovin' Gambler," and "Rye Whiskey," and that old camp meetin' song, "Do, Lord."

We would walk until I felt her muscles relax, felt her breathing change, she would go limp as puddin' and settle into the cradle of my arms, head next to my heart, and then I knew it was time to put her back into bed awhile.

Diane rested some. She began to give over more of the night calls to me, and I took over the predawn shift. Daybreak is the best time for me, the worst for Diane. She would stir but sleep on if she heard me get up and go to Jenny. I soon learned that mother's trick of being able to sleep soundly while listening for the cry in the night.

Then I would gather Jenny into my arms and carry her to a quilt on the floor in the "glass room" at the far end of the cabin. The bedrooms were to one side of the big central room, the glass room was the other wing. It was glass, floor to ceiling, the side facing the creek and down along the long sidewall. The view gave one the feeling of being high in the trees. Here the first rosy light of dawn would rise from the tree line across the creek. Jenny and I would lay ourselves down here. I called this our picnic time.

I would cradle the baby in the crook of my arm, the nursing bottle propped to my chest. I would watch in contentment as she filled her little tank. That's about as close to nursing as a daddy can get.

Breakfast done, bottom dry, daylight coming, Jenny and I would curl up and calm each other. We would look long into each other's eyes. Soon those long golden lashes, so much like her mother's, would begin to flutter, then droop, and come to rest lightly as butterflies on her downy cheek. I could feel her grow calm. She would snuggle in deeper, put an ear to my heartbeat and sleep. I would not have moved for anything.

There Diane would find us when she awoke, rested, in the full light of day.

"Look at you two, all stuck together."

"It's our mess, we can sleep in it if we want to."

Jenny, recognizing the sound of her mother's voice, would reach up to her, smiling. This child had two parents. That may not sound so remarkable, but I missed all the little first times like this with my young man's family. And that is now one of my sharpest regrets. They never lacked love and attention from their mother, but the business of taking time to be a part of an infant's life is optional for the father. Young fathers can be so busy—so dumb.

I remember telling myself then that I would make friends with them when they got older, more human. And the only thing they knew of me was their mother's "Be quiet, your father's sleeping." Which later became "Be good or when your father gets home he'll get you."

I worked hard. My career was a success, but I had no time for little children. I would get to know them later. Not thinking that later they might not have time for me. They hardly knew me.

I really had not much choice about being close to Jenny. Her colic and Diane's fatigue were a clear call to all hands. What surprised me was my coming to like it. It may have been the softening of my years. Partly, yes, but mostly it was the astonishing discovery that there was someone in there from the very first days.

Jenny and I would lie quietly, concentrating on each other's eyes, and enjoy the simplest of games. I would softly say "boo!" and she would break into gales of laughter. Then we would settle down, watching each other intently, building up the moment for "boo" again.

I would simply have never dreamed that it was possible to have some communication, some recognizable game, with a little human who had been here on earth about twenty-one days!

Once while Diane was cooking supper I was dancing in the dark with Jenny out in the glass room. We were slow-dancing, a sort of waltz; I was making up the words as we went along and singing soft and low. Then I became aware of Diane watching us from the other room.

We went on dancing, I told her that dancing with Jenny was no different than dancing with any other beautiful girl, only I didn't have to worry about where my feet were.

In the half-light Diane softly asked, "Then why are those tears running down your cheeks?"

This was the first time I had been something special to a child. I was surprised at how much it meant to me.

CHAPTER 5

Diapers

I never got used to diapers. I think mothers are born with some special immunity to diapers that fathers never acquire. There hasn't yet been a scientific solution to diapers, although a friend of my youth did come close. When his wife would go out and leave him with the baby, he'd put all the dirty diapers into the freezer and save them for her to tend to, the diaper and the contents frozen hard. "I don't like surprises," was his only comment.

As a young man my solution to diapers was simple: I never changed one. "Woman's work," that ghastly old echo of precious years lost. I never bathed a little bottom either nor chased a gleeful runaway naked child.

When Jenny was about a month old and we were just about desperately done in, Diane called her mother and asked if she could come back and help us. Sally stayed six days this time and spread a lot of calm and order over things just being there. She also reduced the "duty watch" by one third and I dated her daughter again. Took her out to eat, although at any lull in the conversation there was no point in asking this beautiful woman across the table from me what she was thinking about.

Jenny was absolutely up to the task of keeping all three of us on the run. She could keep three crews busy: the one who had her right now; the one who was running the washer and the dryer and thinking, Just wait 'till I get that baby in *my* arms, and the one who had just been relieved and gone to the shower in despair and would be expected to come back and fold clothes.

We gave up on cloth diapers, started buying the disposable kind, many boxes of them, then case lots. Sometimes I would just look at Jenny, still so tiny, and think how remarkable her processing capacity was.

At one point I decided that Diane was discarding the disposable diapers too early, not getting efficient use from them. In secret, I tried an experiment for prolonged use of the paper diaper. When the first one came apart in midflight and Jenny showed traces of a rash on her bottom, both ladies looked straight at me. Like veteran cops on the beat, they knew what to expect from whom.

Diane was more relaxed, having more fun. One day I came home and found her and Jenny lying in a swatch of sunlight out in the glass room, stopped in the act of changing a diaper, just lying there, gazing at each other.

"You are playing dolls." I accused my wife. Her only reply was about the dreamiest smile I have ever seen. They relished every moment together.

At other times I would come home, hearing Jenny long before I could get up the stairs, and find Diane with hair matted, blouse pulled nearly backward and baby-food carrots all around. At times I feared that she might give up and run off to Mexico.

At three months Jenny was about the size of an Opelousas catfish and just as slippery. She was slowly getting over the colic, she mostly outgrew it. Diane's health was about back to normal, and the sense of living in some desperate state of emergency was passing from our house. We had all worked as a pretty good team. That was until the day they casually handed me a little box and said, "Here, give Jenny one of these suppositories."

I was aghast.

Jenny knew she had me, too. She lay calm during my gingerly efforts, then the kid closed both eyes, compressed her lips, and fired that suppository at the wall.

Wap!

There was a lot of what I considered unnecessary laughter from the womenfolk. Even Jenny grinned at me. But at last I was a member of this club.

My mother-in-law, wiping away the tears of laughter, said, "Gordon, I take back all the rotten things I've thought about you."

Then Jenny was about four months old and feeling good in the first winter of her life. We don't have much winter on the Texas Gulf Coast, and most of it comes after Christmas. The days were mild and the forest was rich with the golds and reds of turning leaves and our road was carpeted with their color.

It is about a mile down our sandy road to the mailbox, through an arbor of trees. Diane tucked Jenny's blankets in tight and I took her along, this time riding in a little four-wheeled baby carriage. She was getting too hefty to carry that far just in arms.

Diane waved us bye-bye from the cabin door and went back upstairs for at least an hour's peace. Jenny and I shoved off, her eyes watching the bright canopy of trees overhead and the patches of clear sky. The rock and rattle of the buggy soon lulled her into a sound sleep, the nip of Canada in the north winds touching her cheeks with color. When her lips moved in her sleep, a long-forgotten saying of my old Indian grandmother came back to me: "The angels are talking to her in her sleep."

Then a pale-rosy leaf from a Chinese tallow tree spiraled down and came to rest on her coverlet, matching the translucent beauty in her cheeks, and I knew that this moment would be long remembered.

CHAPTER 6

Crossing Jordan

Jenny may have arrived upon this earth a whole person but utterly helpless and totally dependent upon others for her next meal, but God in his infinite wisdom had provided her with an effective signal, sometimes a dreadful weapon, something that made her an equal: her voice.

Like a carborundum circle saw blade that can cut through concrete and steel, ceramic tile or the silence of the night, shatter a row of crystal on the shelf or flatten a cat against the wall, Jenny's voice was something to be reckoned with. I suspect that Jenny in full cry showed up on the local TV radar weather map as a small but intense isolated thunderstorm cell.

Jenny was baptized on December 4, 1977. Every tradition was observed, even the little white christening cap to be folded away and kept for her wedding-day handkerchief; something old. But Jenny had her own ideas about this solemn occasion.

Jenny did not cross Jordan quietly. She went across that mighty river of Christianity at the top of her voice. Jesus, Moses, Abraham and all the heavenly hosts could hear her for miles and miles. The Angel Gabriel must have laid aside his mighty trumpet and cocked his head and listened with professional admiration.

Jenny was wide-eyed and silent as long as the girl kept playing the guitar and singing softly, but when they dipped Jenny's rosy fanny into that water, she really cut loose. She purpled up and stiffened in outrage. There were eight other peaceful little brand-new Christians there who raised their tiny heads and looked around. Who was this kid water-skiing on the River Jordan?

From where I stood, I could tell that the rites were still going on; I could see the pastor's lips still moving. Diane was in a four-handed fight to put Jenny's little white christening dress back on, but before she could do it Jenny warmly baptized Diane. Diane hurriedly passed our child to me and she promptly stuccoed my marryin' and buryin' suit by tossing up lunch on my shoulder, making me an admiral with one fancy epaulet. I gave Jenny back to Diane. She handed me a wet diaper, right there in church. Out in the crowd I could see Jenny's older brothers and sisters trying not to crack up. I rolled up the wet diaper and tossed it over the heads of the other worshipers. An artist friend of ours fielded it; kept it; later he said he was going to give it back to Jenny on her wedding day.

I have been in and out of a lot of close shaves with the church, but nothing like having our daughter Attila the Hun baptized.

Outside in the sunlight, my kids asked me why I hadn't raised one leg, stomped the floor and done "The Wabash Cannonball" with her. I should have.

During this springtime of '78 Diane, Jenny and I coasted into a period of noncrisis, just being people and enjoying each other. Jenny was roly-poly pink, a carpet creeper, pulling herself along, turning over when she wanted to, laughing at her own games. Diane and I were fascinated watching the development of her mind, which seemed to double its capacity with every new day.

I had just gotten the good news that my book *Bax Seat* was being published, and I was spending this quiet time in our lives enjoying springtime on the creekbank and writing about it in a new book, *Village Creek.* I noticed that both Diane and I had quit thinking of Jenny as "the baby." She was a third person in the household, one with her own special likes and dislikes and many ways of expressing her anger or joy over things. Jenny seldom cried now except for a good reason— when she was wet, hungry, or frustrated over something she was trying to do and her little hands and arms just wouldn't yet do all the things her mind wanted them to.

I tried imagining what a towering monster a grown person must look like, standing over a tiny baby on the carpet. So I got down on the carpet to find out if I could see things from her point of view. Eye to eye we went exploring and I discovered her world. The world of carpet microcosm, as fascinating as any sea-floor study.

She could always find straight pins. They drift down unseen and bury themselves in the deep kelp of the carpet. To Jenny they must have looked like big shiny cannon barrels from a sunken treasure ship.

Also unnoticed by lofty surface treaders are the husks of dead bugs. Jenny would discover these and in a quick grab savor them, sometimes offering me halvesies.

At Diane's suggestion I hung a little canvas jumper swing from the central beam in the big room. This gave Jenny a whole new view of things, kept her happy for hours. She would set up a steady thumping rhythm with one sturdy leg, bouncing the chair lightly on its spring, and soon learned to manuever the chair so that she could always be facing Mommy and whatever might be going on in the kitchen. There she would sit for hours, thump thump, cooing little sounds of contentment.

When Jenny was a solid six months, we had our first separation. In early summer, she and Diane went off to visit Diane's family in Dallas.

I was shocked at the stony silences that dropped over my creekbank cabin with nothing gone from there but a little chunk of a girl about two feet tall.

I missed Diane too, but we had worked out ways of being together while apart. Before she left I gave her eight letters, one to be opened each day she was gone. She hid eight notes for me, stuck to the TV dinners in the freezer or under my socks, and one hidden in a pair of her panties, tucked away under my pillow. "Not fair," I cried when she got home. "Just wanted to see if you were making up the bed," she replied with a maidenly smile.

I was late getting home from work on the day of their return and was hurrying to the woods to see my two ladies. It had been a long eight days, and not just the TV dinners. I had decided that when a man is gone he is only the man gone, but when the woman is gone and takes the child with her everything is gone.

Diane was standing under the light at the top of the steps, her hair softly gleaming, Jenny on her hip. Not a word was spoken. I stopped my hurrying and started up the steps one by one toward them, savoring every moment.

Jenny turned and looked. One arm securely around her mother's neck, she was absolutely motionless. I ascended the steps making little daddy sounds. Jenny just stared. For a moment I had the wild thought that she had forgotten me. In just eight days. Then, at the last possible moment, and with the most delicate sense of timing that any actress could possess, she lowered her eyelashes, broke into a big grin, and reached her little arms out for me.

After all the dancing and hugging, the three of us settled down in the big room to "show Daddy all the things you learned at Grandma's." We gathered in a family circle on the carpet, and there was little miss round rump sitting up. Sitting alone, steady, straight up and ready to vote.

Oh, she knew this was good, better than lying around on the rug all day like a little pink alligator. She could shove herself upright, but sometimes she overdid the shoving and went right on over backward.

Jenny was proud of her newfound freedom of movement. I looked at her sturdy little body and my heart brimmed with pride. I ran for the camera to catch studies of her on film. It was a grand time for all of us. I checked in the baby book to see if she was sitting up early, maybe stronger and smarter than average. Even though six months was about average for sitting alone, I still bragged a lot next day to anyone who would listen.

When Jenny had left for Grandma's she was mostly concerned with eating and sleeping and yelling if she needed something. Now suddenly there she sat, a delightful human with dancing eyes, daring me to play games with her.

And she had discovered the wonder of her hands. First one, then the other. Then her hands found each other, clasping, touching, her eyes studying them deeply. I reached out and gave her my hand. She clasped it with her little pink one, touched, grasped, then our eyes would meet in delight at all this.

Soon Jenny found she could fairly well hit what she was swiping at. That she could use her hands to reach far and bring more wonderful new things to her mouth. Looking up, she found me totally absorbed and offered to share. You ever taste a cold, wet, half-dissolved piece of Zwieback? What would you have done, hurt a lady's feelings? She laughed as I munched into the soggy Zwieback, making faces. And I laughed, too.

Granny had also taught Diane that it is OK to just put the baby down now and then. That the yelling, the fist-pounding and the leg-kicking would slowly trail away like a passing summer thunderstorm.

In just eight days with Granny, Jenny had learned to put herself to sleep and to spend hours of the daytime sitting on her quilt, playing alone, babbling and cooing to herself. Jenny did not need one or the other of us every instant. She had crossed some kind of Jordan of her own.

In some ways I missed being a part of the center of Jenny's universe. I know Diane did, too, although we never sat down and talked about it.

It was easy to get a good game going anytime with Jenny. I

would creep off on hands and knees, Jenny watching with delighted eyes, and I would hide behind a chair. Not a sound or a move from either of us. Then "Boo!" I would pounce out of hiding. Jenny would pretend to be surprised and reward me with cackles of laughter, holding out her arms for a hug, before the monster sneaked off behind the furniture to hide and let the suspense build again.

Seeing a playful sense of humor being born in her was beautiful. Even before we shared a common spoken language, we shared laughter—to last her all her life. And in my heart I could see God again. The second thing He gave her after the cry for help was the gift of laughter.

CHAPTER 7

Childproof

The lull of good humor after the trip to Granny's lasted about a month. Jenny would spend hours of contentment in her little jumping-jack chair, getting just enough action out of it with one slowly thumping foot to lull herself to sleep, then sleep there slumped and content while we tippy-toed about the house.

It was during this time that we first heard her deep belly laugh. We had romping kittens, at the skidding-sideways and cutting-flips stage, playing around her feet, sometimes pouncing on them. The sound of laughter would come rolling up from deep inside Jenny. Still does when something great is going on. I hope some parlor politeness, learned later in life, never changes her laugh.

Diane was the first to notice that Jenny was teething. Chewing, gnawing, sometimes fretting. "She's cutting a tooth." Soon Jenny had some kind of rubber or plastic teething ring always within reach, although I think she preferred her own knuckle or the furniture.

It was then that I began to suspect that our Jenny would never float gently down the river of life, serenely meeting each new obstacle. The teething almost drove her wild. And what drove Jenny wild drove Diane wilder. I got so I could look at our cabin from the parking lot and know that things would be shambles upstairs.

One day Diane met me at the door, that tight-wired look around the corners of her eyes.

"What now?"

"She's got a tooth."

Oh my, that's nice. I probed for the tooth, and Jenny, seeking relief, bit my finger with enough force to puncture the lid of a can of infant carrots. "Yeo-ow!"

Jenny looked at me, squirming with the urge to rub, to bite, to gnaw. All around were the discarded teething devices. Diane and I broke into laughter and hugged each other. First tooth! First sign of growing up. Next thing she'd be walking and talking. We were being perfectly silly. Jenny watched us with satisfaction.

Now Jenny began pushing along the floor, traveling, tasting whatever did not move. She was finding out about kitchen cabinet doors that opened up into worlds yet undreamed of. She had discovered electric-light outlets all along the baseboards and was looking for something to plug into them just the way Mommy and Daddy did.

I found her carrying one of Diane's long metal bobby pins, her gaze fixed upon an electrical outlet "Di-aaane!" I bellowed.

Diane appeared with a little box full of snap-on covers for the outlets. "Just as I thought," she said. "I had already bought them."

While we were standing and congratulating each other, Jenny came shoving up and handed me one of the newly installed safety covers. She had just pried it off.

"Omigod."

"Wait," said Diane, and swiftly returned with a bigger box of safety plugs of a much more serious design that I had to install with tools. Some of them will still be there when Jenny comes home from the university, I'll bet.

Diane had also bought "childproof" cabinet latches and they worked just as well, only now it took two of our hands to open any cabinet door. For a time I wondered what ever happened to those good old days of "no," when folks just smacked a kid lightly instead of trying to outsmart her. When, I wondered out loud, do we start teaching Jenny to obey?

It was just dawning on me that we had brought Jenny along this far and I couldn't remember either of us ever laying a hand on her. Spankings would have to begin pretty soon or we'd have a little outlaw among us. A, to coin a phrase, "spoiled brat."

Diane interrupted these dark thoughts. "How did you keep your other kids out of things?"

"I warned them a time or two, then I just let 'em have it." I was trying to soften the way that sounded by grinning a little and lapsing back into thick Texas drawl.

"You warned them a time or two, then you just hit the child?"

It sounded a lot more awful than it really was in that clinical way Diane had of saying it. I decided to let it go for now and indicated from the hardware remaining in my hand that we would be one cabinet short of childproof latching.

"I know. That one out on the end, easiest for her to reach, is Jenny's cabinet. I'll put a lot of pots and pans like mine in there for her to get to. Along with teaching her to respect the rights of others, I want her to learn that she is also entitled to a place for things of her own."

For a fleeting moment I realized I was being led out onto new ground and asked for the wisdom to keep my mouth shut. I also had a fleeting moment of wishing I had had a mommy like Diane.

I put a little safety gate at the head of the inside stairway, and I'm probably the guy who left it open, too. I was downstairs in my workshop, Jenny was upstairs in the kitchen, when Jenny demonstrated to us both that she could travel farther and faster than either of us realized. I heard the unmistakable sound of a soft baby body tumbling down the stairs.

Being the nearer, I got there first. In the split seconds it took to reach her, all of these thoughts tumbled through my mind: being thankful I had carpeted this stairway with a thick pad at the bottom to brush sand off shoes as people came into the house; remembering when I used to roll down my grandmother's stairway just for the fun of it; being more afraid of what-all Diane was going to say than of Jenny's being hurt. Jenny just looked mad and scared and was purpling up to do some real yelling, lying flat on her back on the pad at the bottom of the stairway.

Diane, flying down the stairs, was all business. She knelt beside Jenny, began with careful fingers to feel her all over. I was kneeling beside them, feeling guilty as hell but fairly sure that Jenny wasn't hurt. With the freshly crashed Jenny lying between us, Diane about satisfied that nothing was broken, I said, "She couldn't be hurt too bad with all that wind left in her." Diane looked up at me through Jenny's yelling with just plain fury in her eyes. She didn't say anything. She didn't need to. And I just felt all the more guilty.

Later, when we had all calmed down some, Jenny cradled in her mother's arms on the couch, I sitting beside them, hands in my lap and head down, Diane opened the gates of mercy. She turned to me with a little half-smile and said, "Well, at least she has found out about down." And she began to teach Jenny to say the word: "Down."

I was relieved and thankful that there had been so little damage. But in my mind there ran a jerky horror movie of all the hazards facing Jenny now that she had learned to shove off from the safety of our quilt by the window and into the world.

My worst fear was the beautiful creek running right by the front of our cabin. Village Creek was a child-taker. So many times I had held hands in a sweep of volunteers to find the body of some child who had wandered off from a family picnic. I have vivid memories of my toe touching a body, feeling it roll away with the gentle current, "I found it! " and diving to bring up a limp and still-beautiful little person and staggering up the sandbar to the wails and cries of the circled family.

That was in my mind when I waded into the creek that first

day we brought Jenny home. Oh please God, don't let Village
Creek ever take my child. My mother was a strong swimmer,
as at home in the water as a seal. She taught us and watched
us like a chicken hawk until one day in a formal test we
proved we could swim across the creek and back. My own
first sons and daughters had had to pass this same test before
they could take off their life jackets.

I vowed never to let Jenny out of my sight when she played
in the sunlit shallows at the sandbar edge. Later when she
could walk, she would toddle through the shallows and I
would let her wade into the current-swept deeps along the
bank. I'd see her feet come out from under her and her eyes
roll in terror as I lifted her out. "Dark water is deep water.
Can you say that?" "Dark is deep," she would repeat, with a
wary eye on the dark pools along the edge.

And I resolved that just as soon as possible she would become a strong swimmer, a water-safe child. Jenny was adven-
turous, yet some instinct kept her away from what would
hurt. Still my mind would play my horror movie.

During my horrors I could hear Diane's voice, patiently
teaching Jenny new words, pulling me back to where we
were. Still a baby and a house I could wrap around her to
make her safe.

CHAPTER 8

The Student

Jenny had experimented with sounds and tried to copy our language from her first month. I would watch fascinated as she combined various tones of "oo-oh" and "ah-hh" with appropriate body language. I could almost see the little wheels turning in her infant head.

Diane believed that Jenny could learn as fast as we could teach her, so, like a mother wren bringing morsels of food to the open beak of her fledgling, she was forever bringing bits of teaching into whatever she and Jenny were doing.

I admired this and tried to do it, too, but down on the floor, with Jenny I would get fascinated with sight and touch and soon my mind would be working at the same level as hers. Any serious academic project we may have started would dissolve into giggles and tickles and rolling over and over into laughter at each other. I suspect that if Jenny and I had been left entirely alone, without the influence of her mother, I would have reached Jenny's age instead of her reaching mine.

The belly-traveling Jenny now had access to her own toy box, her own kitchen cabinet and one more thing, her library. With the library, Diane was giving Jenny a true extension of herself.

In those tender first times when Diane and I had exchanged stories of our own childhood memories, she loved to tell me of discovering books at her grandmother's house. Diane's face would change and soften in the delight of telling of the tall glass-fronted bookcase at Grandmother's, an imposing piece of furniture that I came to imagine looking a lot like Grandmother herself. And of the little child Diane lying on the floor before this bookcase carefully leafing through books Grandmother had gotten down for her. "This is when I began to love books," Diane would always say.

I loved the story, compared it to my own, of my mother making her regular weekly trips to the library and bringing home armfuls of books. Of how I was always hushed by the imposing stillness of the library and had found the children's books and the colorful encyclopedias and could be lost in silent wonder there.

Both Diane and I brought to our marriage memories of books and homes where the grown-ups always read. So it should not come as any surprise that before Jenny was born Diane asked me to build a floor-level bookshelf in what would become the baby's room. Jenny had a library before she saw daylight.

Now, at about nine months, Jenny would see us stretched out in peace and comfort with our books and would go shoving her way across carpets to her own bookshelf, get her own book and imitate us. Her first books were big and bright and juiceproof, but long before she was sure whether books were for eating, teething, or something to just look at they had become part of her life. She learned to turn pages, and established an early ritual of asking us to read to her.

I think of this with a full heart. Diane first gave Jenny the gift of life, then opened to her the everlasting world of books. If Jenny becomes the first woman President of the United States, this is where it all got started.

CHAPTER 9

Girl Sleep

By nine months Jenny had achieved some degree of success in two of the social necessities of life here on earth, communication and transportation. And as Jenny got more independent, I lost more and more of my lofty power over her. No more did she sit up and listen just because Daddy was speaking to her. Now she sorted out the message, and if she found it not to her liking she pitched over backward, yelled and drummed her heels on the floor until one of us caved in.

At such times I usually just picked her up and handed her to her mom and said, "Here. There is something the matter with your kid."

No more could we just hang Jenny up in her jumper swing like a pet parrot to coo and jog the day away. Jenny needed a playmate. She made a constant demand on the attention of one or both of us.

Jenny was now a full-fledged third power in the household. The fact was manifested in every way. Even to the way we crossed a familiar room in the dark. Best to use a sort of sliding-foot shuffle in order to locate wooden blocks, small items of furniture shoved into new locations, or any other obstacle that could surprise the unwary in the dark.

At about this time, Diane and I had established House Rule No. 1, "Wake her up and she's yours." And once awake, she was active, demanding. Both of us could sit and watch her quick coordination, marvel at the smooth muscle in her still baby-shaped body, and could almost read her mind by watching her ever alert gaze light up at some new challenge. I had an important advantage: I left for work each day, got into the outside world, came home to rejoice over Jenny. Diane was in the game constantly; all day long, every blessed day.

One night, Jenny finally sung down and sleeping, Diane set two cups of black coffee on the headboard of our bed, the signal to talk.

"I need time out," she said simply.

I looked at her as though I hadn't seen her for a very long time. She looked like the "before" picture in one of those nagging headache ads. She brushed back a strand of hair. Tried a game little smile. "Just a brief time out. Let me check into the little motel where we go to eat supper sometimes. They know us, my being alone there wouldn't raise any eyebrows."

"Oh baby . . ." I began, reaching for her.

She turned a shoulder. "I love you, Gordon, and you know how I feel about the baby, but I need just one night's girl sleep." She looked in my eyes to see if I was understanding. "I want to bring all the books and magazines I haven't had time to read, I want to bring my shampoo and curlers and hair dryer—just to get all the dried grits out of my hair for one night. I want to live like a queen, having them bring steak and coffee to my room." I could tell she had been going over this in her mind for some time. She was trying not to cry.

The best way to respond to Diane at such a time is to get on with the plan. To talk business. Going off for the night would not be easy for her. More and more I realized how badly she needed this break, wondered how I had not known.

Jenny and I agreed that was nothing we couldn't handle. Along with feeding instructions, Diane left a contract posted on the kitchen cabinet which I had to sign and swear to: that I would be careful around the creek and not carry the baby up the ladder onto the roof again. (I had already done that once. Jenny loved it. Diane was very white around the jaws as she called us and watched me carefully backing down the ladder.) The contract went on about not letting the baby out of my sight near the stairways or any other place either.

I helped Diane load the car, sacks of books, her hair curlers and dryer. She drove off looking back at us. I was standing in the doorway, baby on my hip, "Wave bye-bye to yer mommy," I said.

Mutual friends had offered wagers that Diane would be back in the house before Johnny Carson was. I refused such sucker bets. But I listened to our car driving off down the road with a sort of sinking feeling. I swung Jenny around so I could be face to face with her and announced the terms of the new administration. "I am solely in charge here. If for no other reason than that I am bigger and stronger than you are."

Jenny rared back and gave me a long level look.

It was still early afternoon, and I decided that the first order of business would be to put Jenny in touch with the Good Earth. Nine months is too old to not know anything about the real world. Diapers, sheets, blankets, plastic are all right in their place, but sooner or later a person needs to know the real texture of this planet.

Alone with my daughter and feeling both added freedom and added responsibility, I marched out over the squeaking-clean white sands in front of the cabin, down to the sun-warmed clear shallow ponds that lay at the edge of the creek. Jenny was wiggling naked, her favorite state of dress.

I sat her bare bottom down into the inches-deep warm water and was captured by all the expressions that swiftly crossed her face. First the widened eyes and furrows as she raised her brows in surprise. She looked up at me to see if anything this good could possibly be OK.

She understood the look of fun in my face and immediately got down to the business of a serious study of this place. Her brows knitted, her lips parted, ready for her first standard test of anything new: taste it. I let her.

She spit out the first handful of sand and looked at me with the "Help, Dad" eyes. I scooped up water and washed out her mouth, she sitting so motionless that I knew she must have discovered something else.

I let my gaze follow hers. She was staring at her toes, caught in fascination at tiny darting minnows schooling up around her feet, bumping her with their noses. Our eyes met and we broke into laughter. Jenny leaned over and swiped at the minnows, trying to catch one.

The swift little fish scattered, of course, but Jenny had just discovered the fun of swinging a free arm through water outdoors and making a great splash. More great splashing, both arms now, and laughter. Eyes wide open, she splashed water into both of them and turned to me in hurt surprise, both arms out, eyes shut tight, starting to cry.

I reached back, groping for the dry towel I had brought along (as any good mommy would)—and dried her upturned face. Jenny sat in the warm pond again, now squinting her eyes shut as she splashed.

I warned myself not to keep our little strawberry blonde too long out in the sun, its rays made even more intense by the white sand all around us, but in our splendid isolation there was no sense of time running in me at all. We played and splashed in pure and simple pleasure. Another memory to store in my mind forever.

After a short time, Jenny got curious about what was beyond the pond and crawled out, wet and glistening, into the powdery white sand. In an instant she looked like a new-made sugar cookie of a baby. Distressed at having this stuff all over her, she began to wipe it off with an even sandier hand. Again the cry for help. Old Dad dusted her off with the towel.

She was distracted by the end of a pine needle sticking up from the sand, drew it up for a closer look. With the smallest of fingers she traced it, separated the triad of needles, tested it for flexibility, for taste. I don't know how long we sat there totally absorbed in the matter of her first pine needle. Through her eyes I too was seeing for the first time.

I felt the heat on her little shoulders before the sun tinged them, gathered her up and went to the water's edge. She crowed with laughter as I swished her through the shallows for a good desanding. Then as we started up the sandbar toward the cabin she leaned far back in my arms, toward the creek, reaching for more.

We settled onto the cabin's soft carpet, with a clean diaper, and our day passed in peace. I came to an early conclusion that the baby was not so much trouble, that Diane wore herself out with needless and constant work. It was still early.

I made a contract with Jenny that day. A foolish one. I promised her that I would not ask her to eat anything I wouldn't eat. "I will feed you. You can feed me." My plan was to make a game instead of a contest of eating time.

"You feed Daddy, Daddy will feed you. Open your little mouth." She caught onto the game at once. We were eating the baby food that Diane had left for her. Jenny couldn't manage the spoon, of course, so I was getting my share by hand over a pretty wide area from my chin to my nose. From her laughter, Jenny must have decided this was improving my looks.

On her turn Jenny was taking the spoon from me very neatly. Just as I always suspected, the mealtime mess is a game invented by the baby. There is nothing in the world as sure as a one-shot expert.

I also found out that baby oatmeal tastes like wet cardboard, her green beans looked like a bad caterpillar wreck and had no taste at all, and the stuff they serve as veal for babies is unspeakable.

We got tidied up again, and the day resumed its peaceful mood, but I was surprised at how much of it seemed to have already slipped by. I had already noticed that events with the babies come and go in peaks. A peaceful lull was followed by notice of need for another diaper change. A serious one this time. I was being very careful changing the diaper instead of having the cup of coffee I had planned to reward myself with, when the phone rang.

Just as the phone rang the hot-water kettle began to whistle. It all sounded very serious and urgent.

I was foolish enough to turn loose of Jenny with one hand to grab for the phone. Jenny flipped away from me at once, scattering the contents of her diaper, and began finger-painting in it. I began to shout. She began to shout. The phone was still ringing and the kettle still whistling.

I pinned Jenny down with one hand, grabbed the phone and shouted into it, "Call me back!"

Whoever it was never did.

Later in the bathtub, submerged to chin level, both of us calmed down considerably, I realized she was secretly drinking the bathwater. True to my promise, I did that, too. Not as bad as it looks.

I had planned a lot of other projects for our day, but when Jenny gave up and went to sleep, so did I.

I had no idea how I got so exhausted, or where the time went. All day long I was either tending to Jenny or not daring to start something new because I knew I was going to be tending to her again in a minute or so. So I just sat around. The house looked like a battlefield.

It was early dark, Jenny was sleeping lightly, angels watching over her, when I heard the car back in the woods. Any car you can hear has got to be coming here. The road doesn't go anywhere else.

I was standing outside by the front door of the cabin when a shiny-haired rested Diane came creeping in.

"Do you still love me?" she asked. "I couldn't spend the whole night."

I took Diane by the shoulders and looked long and deep into her face. "If you ever leave me . . . I'll come get you," I said.

CHAPTER 10

Vitamins and Minerals

For such a robust, fast-developing baby-child, Jenny seemed to be plagued with an inordinate number of minor illnesses. I watched Diane ministering to her with the latest pills and potions and secretly wondered if Jenny was really OK and Diane was caught up in the doctor game.

It seemed to me that Diane called the doc at every sniffle or whiffle from Jenny, and that he, in order to be worth his salt, would gravely pronounce some new ailment. None of it serious, no fevers, no sores, nothing like when she had colic. Just a constant running diagnosis. Read too many medical books and the same thing could happen to you, was my own private diagnosis which I kept to myself.

At about ten months Jenny could briskly crab-crawl across the room and pull up on things and stand there on sturdy little legs. She could shove herself upright when she came to an obstacle in her pathway, and she knew this was good. Holding on with both hands and chortling with delight, she would look around to be sure one of us was watching. She wanted our approval and she wanted our attention. I was starting to wonder if there was ever going to be any relief from either "Look at the baby" or "I wonder what's the matter with the baby."

One thing for sure, I wasn't safe in my Daddy chair anymore. When I got home from work, fell out with a sigh and a cup of coffee, Jenny would make a beeline for me, pull up on my chair and, if I tried to just pat her head and go on reading the paper, play wreck-the-paper with however much of it she could get a grab at.

If I moved to the table to sort the day's mail instead, Jenny would pull up on the table with her "Hey, look at me!" crowing and there was nothing to do but play. I made paper airplanes out of the fallout from the day's mail and sailed them to her. Jenny was fast becoming a child, ready or not.

Diane tried to help by telling her, "Not now, your daddy's too tired," but that brought back all the bad ghosts of the kind of daddy I was before. I managed to work it out by just accepting and rejoicing that Jenny was glad to see me when I got home. She would come at me like a little warm cannon-ball, and I would drop everything and join her in some silly game. Her attention span was short enough that she soon had enough of the novelty of my being home and would think of something else to do and crawl happily away. I had the love and affection of this little person now. Don't waste any of it, I warned me.

But I hung on to my own prejudice that Diane was over-mothering her, and tried to be understanding.

Sometimes Jenny would cry out in her sleep. I didn't take it seriously, but Diane went over her like a mother monkey. Her pronouncement: Jenny had an earache.

Back to the doctor's office we went, with this little child so rosy with health and me full of hidden doubts. The doctor's report was that Jenny had a severe and painful ear infection, probably caused by some allergy, and that if left unchecked it could result in permanent hearing loss.

Diane turned and looked straight into me with her mind-reading eyes. She knew what I had been thinking all along, of course.

The allergy diagnosis was not easy for me to accept. I do not believe in allergies. I told her so after we got home. In my best Old Navy quarterdeck voice, and striking a commanding pose to go with it, I said, "There will be no allergies in this house. I forbid it."

Diane made no immediate reply. She gave me a blue-steel sighting look that would have made a great picture for the National Rifle Association, captioned "Winner, Women's Division, heavy-caliber rifles."

I was not afraid. I went on, forcefully telling her how it was when my little brother Tom and I were brought up during the Great Depression. We were too poor to have allergies. Only rich folks' kids had allergies.

Tom and I were never sick. We were left out in the rain, nourished on a steady diet of peanut-butter sandwiches and sometimes bologna. We got plenty of milk. Not that funny pasteurized stuff, but real honest raw milk from Ida, Grandpa's cow. Grandma milked her and carefully strained the milk for any floaties or little black specks. You could look at it and see that it was clean. If Ida got her foot into the milk bucket, we never drank the milk no matter how hard times were.

Tommy and I never caught cold. If the dog licked our sandwich we ate it anyway. It was our dog. We shed germs. There was no new germ that could make any headway against all the germs we were full of all the time.

Oh, we had heard of allergies. There was one little rich kid, who used to come out from town to play with us. "Peaches 'n Cream," we called him. He had that pale look, that fine translucent skin at the back of his knees. He was an allergy kid. Not fit to play with. If Tommy or I fell out of the top of a tall tree we were expected to get well. This kid always had something the matter with him and was not allowed to climb trees. We would wait until his high-heeled, tight-skirted mother got through hovering over him, then we would secretly torture him. Nothing bad, never left any marks.

"I'll bet you and Tommy had runny noses all winter," Diane said.

"We had long sleeves in the winter," I replied.

Actually there was one recognized disease we had in the

winter. We called it "Indian Fire." You never hear of a kid getting Indian Fire anymore. It was a long continuous scabbing, itching, oozing of the shin area. To pull up your overalls leg and slowly reveal a good case of Indian Fire, all red and yellow and oozy, was worse than seeing the *Frankenstein* movie. A kid gave me a nickle one day to do it in class. Two or three little girls had to be excused.

Some folks tried to tell me later in life that Indian Fire was a form of allergy. Well, we didn't know it then and I'm going to be ironheaded about believing it now.

Diane sat and listened to my whole outburst on allergies, correctly graded it as mostly storytelling, and went on with allergy testing for Jenny and herself too. Not believing in allergies, I didn't need any.

Diane and Jenny would sit for hours with all those other wretched kids and their mammas in the waiting room of that allergy clinic, then they would get a needle-prick test for their reaction to every food in the supermarket and most of everything else on earth. We got Jenny okayed for a diet of strained sow snouts and cream of mockingbird livers. Diane said sarcasm didn't help.

But Jenny did have a most depressing list of sensitivities to everything good to eat, the dust of the earth, the trees in the sky. For where we lived in the forest, that sounded about as impossible as having a New York City kid who was allergic to cement sidewalks.

Diane cheerfully took up the tasks of trying to make the house dust-free and preparing the special diet for both herself and Jenny. Later they both got special allergy shots. Jenny's ear infections began to improve immediately and were cured eventually. Diane, who had suffered from headaches and some form of bronchitis, also got better. And both of them became remarkably free of colds. And I must admit to being thankful for a watchful mother who knew almost as soon as the baby did that her ear was hurting.

It was during this trying time of allergies that our elegant Fleetwood Keats came down with a mysterious scurvy of the fur. Keats was a beautiful tortoiseshell tom, a longhair with white underbelly and boots and a most expressive plume of a tail. He had come into our world during the times before our baby did, when Diane's love-starved arms wanted something to carry and to cuddle. No tomcat had a better life. All he had to do was put up with being carried around feet up and baby-talked to all day. When Jenny was born Diane put the cat down.

Keats's thick hair began to fall out along his center line. His once expressive tail shed away to a bare and awful-looking appendage that not even a possum would carry. Keats grieved. We all grieved.

After several tries with several vets, Diane found the one whose diagnosis seemed the most believable. "Sibling rivalry," said the doctor of veterinary medicine without cracking a smile. This agreed with what Diane had known all along. We were to give Keats birth control pills for his hormone imbalance.

You ever try to give birth control pills to a full-grown, battle-wise tomcat? Don't laugh. I still have some of the slash marks.

The big stupid tomcat began to leaf out again, but would still sit and look moon-eyed at Diane with the baby in her arms. When Diane first told me of the turmoil in his soul and that was causing him to lose his fur, I got up without a word, went into the bathroom, leaving the door open, was gone a long time. Curiosity at last got the better of Diane. She peeked in the door. There I was, in front of the mirror, holding a hand mirror, trying to see if the fur had starting falling off my center line yet.

"What am I doing?" she asked, "Living with three babies?"

"Me-owww," I meowed.

The vet later gave Diane a thick, goopy-looking solution in a small bottle with an eyedropper to get Keats's new medicine down his throat. She had at least one kind of medicine for Jenny to be taken the same way. We settled into this new routine of medicating kid, cat and wife until one sleep-fogged

morning when Diane had all her medication and all her un-
willing patients lined up. In the struggle I heard Diane cry
out, "Omigod!" She had poked a big eyedropperful of the
black goop down Jenny's throat and squirted the tomcat full
of Jenny's vitamins.

I bounded into the kitchen, where they were all still caught
in a frozen tableau of astonishment. Then the cat got away,
leaving long toenail marks on the flooring, Jenny caught her
breath and yowled, and Diane trampled me on the way to the
phone. It was early on a fine Sunday morning.

When she came back, still ruffled, Diane's only comment
was that she planned to find another vet because no doctor
could be trusted who would laugh hilariously over the phone
while assuring her that neither kid nor cat had been hurt by
each other's medication. "And I woke him up, too, and him
laughing like that." Diane shook her head.

While Diane continued religiously with her treatments of
vitamins and minerals on whoever she could catch, a lush
springtime settled over our creekbank cabin. It may be hard
to believe that any part of Texas could be like a jungle, but
deep in the southeast corner where we lived is an area called
the Big Thicket. Most of the forest here is now the Big
Thicket National Park, a preserve of the rare ferns and fauna
growing in this double-canopied rain forest. Here cactus and
wild orchids grow side by side. Nature's "lapland," where the
cool dry Canadian winds are lapped over by the warm, wet
tropical winds off the Gulf of Mexico. A beautiful place, and a
true jungle.

Out of the dense vines of each changing season comes a
great hatching of new larvae. There are swarms of whatever
bug the larvae turn out to be, until the other bugs and birds
thin them down some. "Bug of the month," we call this phe-
nomenon.

In May of '78 the bug of the month was a pale fuzzy worm,
just under an inch long, on the way to becoming a swarm of

mayflies. The mayworm was a dropper out of trees, a collar rider into the house, a carpet creeper. Jenny and the mayworm developed as carpet creepers at about the same time.

Closer to the carpet than we, and with perfect vision, Jenny could easily overtake a mayworm. If she beat Diane to it in the race, the little caterpiggle just vanished.

Diane shuddered. She mounted on all-out carpet police campaign. But she never considered the fine white marble urn that stood about a foot and a half tall and graced our doorway. Or why Jenny loved to pull up to that urn and stand there content beside it, a picture of grace and beauty in the fine morning light.

Diane was becoming not only wise to the various yowls and yells from Jenny, but also very wary of any silence that lasted too long. And thus it was that she came to investigate and found our little cherub of the marble urn standing bright-eyed and balanced beside it, fishing around down inside the urn with her free hand. The shallow slick cavity inside the urn had become a mayworm trap. A cache for Jenny. Diane got there just in time to see one, frantically twisting its little white fuzzy tail, disappear between her daughter's rosebud lips.

"Gor-*don!*" she called. The true emergency cry. I came flying to her side. Jenny, not sure of what this was all about, burst into tears.

Even after the reassuring phone call to the doctor, Diane was still upset. Shuddering and hugging the bewildered Jenny. So I offered my own help. "Diane," I comforted her, "small caterpillars are very high in protein. And they are all vitamins and minerals too. Even the small amount of fuzzy stuff should provide some roughage."

Would you believe that this gentle woman, joined to me in holy matrimony, shook her small white knuckled fist under my nose?

CHAPTER 11

First Step

Jenny took her first step the day before her first birthday, on the day I got fired from the radio station.

Being fired from a radio station is not all that bad, not like being fired from a real job. For thirty-two years I had been the morning mouth of Beaumont, complete with a loyal following of listeners and sponsors. As I bounced back and forth from station to station they went with me. My show was a sort of living soap opera. I shared Jenny and Diane and the stuff of our lives with them, they shared theirs with me. There is one like me in almost every town.

But firing is firing, and even though I had a good offer of another job I came home that day with a bad case of the pitifuls.

As we sat on the long couch, Diane listening with compassion to my story, Jenny was cruising the coffee table in front of the couch. "Cruising," that's what the books call it. What a delightful term. It means the child is old enough now to stand erect, take cautious side steps and cruise around the edge of things, fingers barely touching. Jenny took one more side step at my end of the coffee table and found herself standing alone.

Just stood there, perfectly balanced, not aware. Diane and I tried to keep some kind of talk going so as not to distract

Jenny with the sudden silence. Casually I extended my hand out toward her, but not far enough.

Jenny looked at my hand, at my face, sort of grinned and took her first step alone. Caught my hand and walked surely to the edge of the couch.

There was hollering, laughing, hugging, and a very puzzled but delighted Jenny. And wouldn't you know it, at that moment I couldn't find the camera. And she wouldn't do it again once I did.

Diane was on the long-distance phone, calling her mother in Dallas, spreading all our joy to Granny's house.

After Diane hung up I said, "You forgot to tell her I got fired today."

"Oh. That."

I tried not to sulk right there in the middle of Jenny's first step, but it was not the first time I had felt the sharp barb of jealousy. There was no doubt in my mind that I was no longer the center of Diane's universe. There were even times when I watched her hovering over the baby and that wretched cat Keats and got the sure but skewed idea that in the pecking order of things around here I was third and last.

Now Diane was holding Jenny's hand with just two fingertips and they were walking all around the room. Really struttin' it out, Jenny with that rich full belly laugh of hers as she went.

Diane felt my sulk, came back and put her arms around me. "How many babies am I raising?" she asked again.

"Two. Not counting that scurvy cat. And don't you ever forget it," I said.

"Aw-w c'mon, Gordon, just look at her." And I was drawn back into the circle of things.

Jenny pranced and showed off for us until she was almost asleep on her feet. After she was in bed, Diane and I held each other close. I told her it seemed to me that those first chunky footsteps were laid down on our carpet in solid gold. Then we talked softly in wondrous words of where those footprints might go by the year 2000.

CHAPTER 12

Not Just a Girl

Once Jenny could walk she wanted to run. I suspected that once she could run she'd want to fly, such was our daughter's zest for life. She never crawled again once she knew she could walk. Oh, she tripped and fell a lot, but with an eager eye on her goal she seldom stopped to cry. She just got up and was gone again. Diane and I sat and watched, full of satisfaction beyond words.

For Jenny's first birthday Diane served the traditional birthday cake, one bright candle right in the middle of a little white cake. Blowing out the candle and making a wish were a little too sophisticated for Jenny, but her method of dealing with a mouth-watering cake was right to the point. Jenny got the go-ahead from her mom, reached out, grabbed two fistfuls of cake and crammed as much of it as she could into a happy mouth.

So many of us will never feel the satisfying squish of a handful of cake, or inhale the full bouquet of white icing rubbed plentifully under the nose! The sound of her laughter was the sound of pure pleasure, rich and real.

Jenny at one year was curious about all things, wanted to watch or to help with anything Diane or I was doing. "At this age she is innocent of any idea that she is supposed to be a little girl. That's sort of wonderful. Let's keep it that way as long as we can. Let her play with dolls *and* trucks." So, just as Diane let Jenny get into things with her in the kitchen, I took her with me too when I had something to do down in my little shop.

Diane handed me a little electric fan that needed to be cleaned up and brought back to life now that summer's heat lay over our wooded swampland like a woolen blanket. Instead of dissecting the fan on my workbench I sat down with it on the shop floor so that Jenny could get into it, too.

Jenny was not the only one learning here. I was entering into places with a child where I had never been before. I had taken Jenny into my world. Why not? She was not just a girl.

I started saying out loud the names of the tools I was using. Jenny would pick up the tools and try to say the same word. "Pips" might be an even better name for the Phillips head screwdriver. Who knows?

Jenny's attention to this detail work was short but intense. She had to touch and taste all the fan parts and tools, then she wandered around babbling to herself, exploring the rest of the shop. I worried and was watchful as she picked up the screwdriver with her not yet fully coordinated little arm movements. But I kept quiet.

Among the small nuts and bolts and washers from the fan, there lay my open pocketknife. I had read somewhere that among primitive tribes, where the babies are carried and hugged a lot, they are said to know which objects are dangerous and to leave them alone. Never touched spear points. Jenny didn't either. She seemed to know.

After the fan was cleaned and balanced and a new switch installed to replace the faulty one, I discovered that most of the nuts and washers were missing. Work stopped. I looked at Jenny. She looked at me with her clear steady blue eyes. I held my hand out under her chin. She gave me back the missing parts. Warm, wet, but all there. She smiled. I thanked her.

CHAPTER 13

Boat Oars

Jenny was a little over a year old, in the second vivid autumn of her life with no memory of the first one. I bought a little backpack and began to carry her along on the days when I walked the mile down our woods road to the mailbox.

Sometimes we would leave the winding road and take a shortcut through the forest wilderness. She loved this. She liked to ride high, babbling in my ear as we made our way beneath the trees through the Big Thicket.

I would stop at a huge cypress standing in the low ground and we would look up, following its great trunk high into the sky. I would place my hand on its rough trunk and say, "Tree. Can you say 'tree'?" Then I would turn my shoulders so that Jenny could touch it from the backpack. "Ree," she would say.

Then we would move on to the "o-oos" and "ah-hhs" of bright birds or the quick flush of a rabbit.

We walked through shadows and light, through red leaves and into deep glens, she patting time to my pace with a hand on my shoulder. At the mailbox she knew she could get down out of the backpack, toddle around or crawl into the drifts of bright dead leaves, tossing them into the air. On the way back she always nodded off. Her little head would come forward and snuggle against my neck, and her breath was warm and moist on me. A peaceful time. A primitive time, this man and his sleeping child, passing through the untouched forest. How simple to say now, "Daddy will take care of you."

Other times we went to the mailbox by way of the creek, rowing the little aluminum skiff. This was the slowest way to go. I have a small outboard motor, but if time is no object I would rather row. Oars are one of man's best inventions. The beginnings are lost in maritime history, but no improvements have been made on oars. The last ones are as good as the first.

In the dry autumns the creek was shallow, about ankle deep over clear sand in many places. I would wrap Jenny in a baby blanket and lay her on the transom seat of the skiff, facing the rowing thwart.

Slowly we would make our way upstream, keeping over to the eddy side, the inside of the bends, to stay out of the current. Gliding over white sandbars in amber-colored water reflecting the sky. There was small turbulence passing through the Pillars of Hercules—our grand name for the twin cypress trees that grow midstream. I would bend harder into the oars. Then we saw the low swooping flight of a kingfisher. I told Jenny that to see a kingfisher at the outset of a voyage is an old sailor's omen of good fortune.

As we passed Gaspard's place, his flock of tame ducks steamed out in a grand flotilla to investigate us. Jenny tried to say "Quack quack," watching my mouth as I said it. Suddenly a pair of wild ducks who had been masquerading in Gaspard's flock hoping for a free lunch broke water and, with wings beating twin trails down the placid creek, rose powerfully and banked away in swift flight. Jenny's eyes and her mouth formed perfect O's.

Soon the steady chuck-a-luck of the oar strokes left a little golden head nodding. I rowed on in the utmost satisfaction, watching over the tree line the approach of a mild Texas "blue norther." I beached us in a little sandy cove near the mailboxes, and Jenny and I made the quick trip ashore and back with the mail plastic-bagged and ready for whatever the weather was about to do. We were loafing back downstream when the purple clouds came rollling overhead, a sudden chilly north wind searched us and the first fat raindrops came plopping into the creek all around us.

Jenny's eyes popped wide open. "What's this, Dad?" At first she tried to reach out and touch the little water castles that each raindrop left in the creek, then the pines bowed their tops and the wind was up and rain hissed across the water and drummed in the skiff. I loved it.

Jenny hugged herself, looked at me with the question in her eyes, "Are you sure this is all right?" Her hair was dark wet now, matting her brow. Below it a tight little chin was starting to quiver. Dad sang. He sang mightily over the sounds of the storm and bent to the oars. Downwind and downstream the running skiff fairly flew around each bend, past each sandbar, leaving a chortling wake under her transom. Jenny's brow clouded as she tried to believe she was having as much fun as Dad. But little girls, like kittens, are supposed to be kept warm and dry.

I boated the oars, leaned over and gathered her up off the transom seat, put her astraddle my lap under my blue denim shirt and buttoned the shirt over her. Only her head was peeking out, under my chin. She pulled her hands in to her chest, sighed and endured, a little woman-child made of the same flexible steel as her womenfolk ancestors who came here only a hundred years before huddled in westbound wagons.

Nearly dry and plenty warm, Jenny went back to sleep. I kept singing to the long water-strider strokes of my oars. Another of those times to remember forever.

Then we were shooting the Pillars of Hercules; home was right around the next bend. I called her name softly, "Jenny . . . Jenny, wake up, hon, and look. Who is that?" I turned my body so that she could see ahead of the skiff through the slackening rain.

There was a little lighthouse figure standing solidly in the rain on the upstream end of our sandbar. Jenny looked. "Mommy!"

"Way enough. Boat oars." The slithering crunch of the skiff

riding up onto the sand. There was a great reaching out of arms, I handed Jenny up to her mom, a burrowing to find warm places.

Diane's eyes were glistening in the rain. "You two . . ." she began, then let the rest of it trail off.

CHAPTER 14

Hit the Child?

Jenny was approaching the delightful age of eighteen months. Overalls and twin red pigtails, more a child now than a baby. Our life was sweet, but there was a change in Jenny that was becoming more and more unsettling to me. If either of us told her something she didn't want to do she would just stand spraddle-legged and defiant, put her little hands on her hips, give her pigtails a toss and say, "No!"

She now had a spoken vocabulary of about a hundred words, about ninety-nine of which she kept in reserve. Increasingly she was developing a temper to match the legend of redheads.

Diane seemed strangely serene about all this. Not I. During my own childhood back in the 1920s and the raising of my first family in the 1950s, parental discipline was swift and sure. One of the first things children learned was obedience. The lesson was taught with a good spanking, followed by holding the child tenderly and explaining what the spanking was for. To reassure them that the hand that had blistered their little bottom was still the hand of love.

"Corporal punishment," replied Diane. "A child can be taught to obey with love. It just takes a little longer." There was hard defiance in her soft words. "I don't believe in hitting the child."

"Hitting the child? Good grief, an orderly spanking is not hitting the child. You make it sound awful." I was being driven into a corner with language. Diane sat calmly smiling, but with agate eyes.

I tried logic and reason, her game. "I know you have read a lot of books, Diane, but I raised a lot of children."

A thin film of ice seemed to form over her eyes. No, that was not going to do it.

"Look, Diane, Jenny is too young for reasoning but not too young to need some kind of guidance and control."

That was not even good enough to get a response out of her. I could feel my face flushing. "I was fair and just with my kids, just as my father was before me. They were rewarded if they did good, punished if they did bad. Just as in the real world."

I paused for her nod of agreement. She didn't give it.

"Let me give you an example," I floundered on. "I had one daughter who was bright in school but a talker. I had promised all of them a silver dollar for every A they brought home, but a spanking if they got an F in conduct. Poor conduct is disobedience, you know."

Diane just stared at me. I felt the flood of cold desperation but had to go on with this now. "One day this little girl brought home six A's but an F in conduct. I praised her before the others, gave her the six silver dollars and posted her report card on the wall as was the custom. Then I took her to her room for the spanking. Everybody understood."

I stopped to see whether Diane understood.

She broke her long silence. "I think that is the most cruel and insane story I ever heard."

I cracked. Shouted, "Well, none of them ever spent a night in jail!"

"There are better ways to do it." Diane said softly.

I thought of the hopelessness of Diane's way. Jenny would make a full-arm sweep of all the baby food Diane had lined up on the tray of the high chair. Crash! Splat! All of it on the floor.

Jenny would laugh as Diane cleaned up the mess and put it all back on the tray while explaining in sweetly reasonable tones that we cannot tolerate this kind of conduct, can we?

Jenny would watch her craftily, as if playing a game. Then, crash! All of it swept back onto the kitchen floor again. And why not? Jenny had nothing to fear in life. Not from Diane, not from me.

Oddly enough it was in the high chair that I had first taught my other children the meaning of the word "no." If they reached for their food, whammo! I brought my hand crashing down on theirs. "No!" More noise and surprise than hurt. But in a short time I could say "No" to a child and turn my back on a tray of food. Just like a lion tamer, I thought then.

Diane would put all the food back on the tray, firmly telling the little despot about the wrongness of such conduct, but never laying a hand on her. A year and a half old and getting bullheaded, never spanked and not likely to ever be. I burned with resentment and frustration. Nothing to do but wait and see how this child turned out. Try to tame this one the old-fashioned way and I would have mamma lion all over me.

So I never "struck the child," although my hand itched to. I developed other ways of letting her know not to push Daddy too far. I would growl and look terribly fierce or would crack my voice at her like a whip or snatch her up and carry her to bed in the middle of one of her tantrums and set her down in a way that rattled the teddy bears.

Jenny quickly learned that Mommy and Daddy required separate and different handling. She learned that Mom was safer than Dad. She also learned that Dad was mostly just louder than Mom. It took a little extra twinkling, but Dad could be trained to pick up and hug just like Mom.

This gave me a few things to meditate on. Diane was manipulating Jenny's behavior by love. If I'm not mistaken, the little girl was doing the same thing to me. I felt like an old cannon in the park, silent now for children to play on.

Once or twice when she thought if was safe to talk about such things with me, Diane asked me about my raising of my first family. On a moonlit night, lying abed and watching the creek sparkle between the trees, she asked, "Didn't you find that there were eventually some limitations to power?"

"Power?" Her term for teaching obedience.

"You could only do it because you were bigger than they were," she said. "What did you do after your sons got to be teenagers? Bigger than you."

"I had a Smith & Wesson K-22 pistol, loaded with rat shot. They told me after they had grown up that they never doubted I would use it on them."

"Aw, c'mon, General Patton, was there ever a time when you ran out of power?"

I had to think back. To remember some times I had shut out of my memory.

"Yes, I guess there was one time when my system broke under its own weight. My son was a teenager, had his driver's license, but he kept breaking curfew. I would ground him, put him in hack—that's Old Navy for an officer confined to his quarters and relieved of all duty. I would let him out, he'd be late again. After a time of this he had accumulated so much hack time that he'd be drawing social security before he ever got the car keys back again. He was depressed. So was I. I went for professional help. I asked the counselor, 'What can I expect next?'

"The counselor, an old family friend who had a clear way of expressing himself, said, 'Next he will go out the window.'

" 'What are my choices?' I asked.

" 'Just give him back the car keys, put your arms around the big lout and tell him how much you love him.' "

There was some silence, looking at the creek and recalling the scene.

"Is that what you did?" asked Diane.

I told her it was, and added that this was the beginning of a new closeness between my son and me and he was good about doing what he said he'd do after that.

"That's love," said Diane softly in the dark. "He loves you an awful lot today, too."

"I guess you're right," I mumbled, "but we sure are going to have a time of it with this sassy little girl."

"We'll see," said Diane in the same patient and loving voice that she uses when she is trying to teach Jenny something.

CHAPTER 15

House Husband

I always thought paradise on earth would be to have a job that allowed me to stay home. Work when I wanted to, sleep as late as I wanted to, be with my family as much as I wanted to. If that's paradise on earth, then man may not yet be ready for paradise.

After my firing on Jenny's first birthday I had gotten on as the weekend man on KLVI radio in Beaumont. It's a big old powerhouse of a station, still owned by the Hicks family. They gave me the run of my show and I was able to earn enough to supplement my writing income and live without fear. And I had the whole week free to lie out on the creek and write. No bells to answer.

It wasn't working. Too much togetherness. There was no way I could convince little Jenny that Daddy at the type-writer was not Daddy any other time. I asked Diane to explain to her that when Daddy was writing she had to leave me alone. So instead of her bursting in on me full of laughter and fun, she would tiptoe into the glass room where my office was and silently tap me on the elbow from behind.

That did it. I would snatch the paper out of the typewriter, wad it into a ball and throw it at her. Peals of laughter. Soon she had many balls of white paper to play with all over the rug and I would be out pacing the sandbar, hands jammed into my pockets, head down, trying to get the elusive bird of writing to come perch on my shoulder again.

I was angry with myself for being angry with a loving child, and angry with Diane because we were raising Jenny in such a way that we had no immediate control over her. And angry with Diane for the anger I anticipated she would feel toward me if I brought all that up again. Diane would get angry with me for getting angry with her when she was not angry with me. And all this from the tap of a little pink finger from a child who shared everything else with Dad and couldn't understand why she couldn't play with him now.

These were difficult times.

Ironically the book I was writing was about the idyllic life on Village Creek. The problem was, it was coming at me faster than I could find a lull in which to write about it.

Then one night after Jenny was asleep, Diane approached me as if she were holding two sticks of dynamite only they were two cups of coffee. She was giving me the signal that another serious family council was being called to order.

I wanted to reach out, gather her to my arms and assure her by my very presence that she was safe, all was well, and tell her how beautiful and big and round her eyes are. Diane was not to be deterred by such simple flimflammery. Congress was in session.

"Gordon," she said, looking straight at me with the same expression as the prisoner telling the commander of the firing squad never mind the blindfold, "what would you think of my taking a job. Going to work?"

I did everything I could to hide what I really thought about that. What I really thought was straight out of the nineteenth century, just like the rest of me: Show me a working wife and I'll show you a failed husband. That's what I thought about that.

The thought flashed through my mind so fast and on such a well-worn track that not a trace of it betrayed me. I was able, instead, to gather up my new and ill-formed modern thinking. Diane is of the twentieth century, we are in the twentieth century, I might as well have another sip of it and see how it goes.

"I think it's a great idea." I was able to say honestly. "You've worked most of your adult life. I wondered if dishpans and diapers would be enough for a mind like yours." Careful, Bax, she has her fine-tuned close-range radar thrown over you right now. You could blow it by too much grinning. I decided to move instantly, answering her question with a question, one of the best ploys in the world.

"Do you have any leads? What do you have in mind? Are you going to retrain for office work, or have a shot at going back to the airlines now that the union has opened up the way for married women?"

None of the above. A friend of the family who runs a small CPA office had offered her part-time work as a trainee. "Best of all, he said I can have open hours. I can still be here when you or Jenny need me."

Her face was bright, full of life. There were lights in her eyes. I began to pick up some of her excitement.

"He said one conscientious learner would be worth more than a young college student doing her nails."

He knew Diane. She has a native skill with numbers; a linear thinker. Diane can look over your shoulder and win whatever board game you may be playing. One time she beat me at chess in three moves. She is our family accountant too. She worked with this CPA in making a serious project of my scattered incomes as a free lancer and saved us several thousand legal tax dollars the first year she took over the mess from me. Our CPA noticed then that Diane was a quick study.

As a symbol of my support I went out and bought a leather briefcase for Diane, an open-top model with stand-up carrying handles. She loved it. Somehow had it loaded the first day, still uses it.

I asked her to start teaching me to cook. "The breadwinner should come home to a hot meal," said I.

She began by teaching me to make white sauce. "The secret of good cooking begins with knowing how to make a good white sauce. You build outward from there."

We enjoyed the times at the stove, shoulder to shoulder, Jenny always nearby, enjoying the peace radiating from us. "Vegetables get bigger. Meat gets smaller," said Diane, passing along ancient basics.

It was slow going for me.

"Courage, you must have courage. Elan! Plunge right in." But uncooked food still intimidated me. She loves salads, and I found my true creative spirit in the bold and artistic salad maker within myself. There is no panic in salad making. Nothing is about to boil over, stick to the pot or burst into smoke and flames during nice cool salad making.

I had newfound admiration for the delicate art and timing of getting a good meal together and onto the table with the phone ringing and the baby calling. But I never learned to be much of a cook.

Good cooks are born, not made, I decided.

Diane truly appreciated the serious effort I was making in our role reversal. Meanwhile, her progress at the office was no less than what I expected.

With her natural drive and attention to detail she rose from trainee to office manager in three months, and without creating any job-threatening questions between herself, the bookkeeper and the accountant who already worked there. In fact, she made new friends of them. She would come home at day's end, face flushed with happiness, pick up the reaching Jenny, gather us about her and tell us how her day went.

She enjoyed being out of the woods and with people again. She enjoyed her work. Happy Diane. I asked if she got flirted with much. "A woman only gets flirted with as much as she wants to," she said primly, "and I have a good man at home."

A good man at home. Oh lordy, that's me.

Jenny and I would stand aside each morning as Diane went through the flurry of getting ready for work. Still looking as though we had just crawled out of bed, we would go down to the car with Diane, who was now all perfect and beautiful and smelling good. She would give us both a quick goodbye kiss. "Mind your daddy. I love you both."

"Say bye-bye to yer mommy," I would repeat in my most

illiterate way, and Diane would whoosh away, leaving us in the silences of the cabin on Village Creek.

"Well, just me and you, kid."

"Let's play, Daddy."

I would gather up this still-warm little cuddlebug, still in her sleepers, and carry her up the stairs to the now utterly quiet house and look around at the things to be done.

Breakfast for us first, with Jenny helping. Then clean up the house, trying to get Jenny to help. Then if I could get her distracted long enough or explain it to her well enough, I would have some golden hours to write.

Jenny was quieter with Diane gone, and I could ask her to play by herself and she would. Diane, I decided, brings a certain amount of excitement with her.

Jenny and I would stand there in the bird-singing cool early light of the day and I would think, So this is what it's like? Easiest of all would have been to just fall back into the bed instead of making it up. As a housewife I would have been a bum.

Diane once asked what Jenny and I did all day, and I honestly couldn't tell her. There was some playing, wading out on the creekfront and looking at bird tracks to see who'd been visiting last night. Coon tracks, snake tracks, turtle tracks, rabbits, mice—the smooth sand was a bulletin board that everyone left a message on.

Then there was lunch, and I must admit that the best way to get Jenny down for naptime was to set her a good example. And then there was always just plain housework. Simple chores, easily done, with my mind left free for writing ahead. I liked housework. I could spend an hour or so at it, then look around and see that something had been done. Things were improved. Most of man's work is not that visible.

I was surprised at how easily I became a pretty good house husband. One midmorning a couple of my kids came by and found me still in apron, sweeping. I explained to them that all that hoo-hawing and rolling over and over on the floor was not going to win them any Oscar. No coffee either. At least I had proof, here in my midfifties, that I had not become set and rigid in my thinking and behavior.

Starting about the time she woke up from her afternoon nap, Jenny would begin asking where was Mommy and when would she be home? We went through this every day until at last I would hear the welcome sound of Diane's car coming through the woods.

"Listen, Jenny. Who's that?"

"Mommy!" And her face would light up and she would tug me to the stairway so we could meet Diane downstairs.

Sometimes we would hurry to pick the late-blooming wildflowers and arrange them with holly and bay leaves that grew in profusion around the cabin, and start down the road to meet Mommy coming in.

The days went along well enough. Jenny and I enjoyed each other and she gave me time to get enough writing done each day. But toward coming-home time, both of us were pulled like the tide toward the sandy woods road that would bring Diane back to us.

CHAPTER 16

Institutionalized

Diane had planned all along that when she became a working mother we would put Jenny into a day school. All she was waiting for was for Jenny to reach the minimum age of eighteen months.

On March 26, 1978, she took Jenny with her when she left for work in the morning, and dropped her off at the day school in Beaumont. Both of them were all prettied up, Jenny proudly carrying her first little adult-world lunch box. Diane was still working open hours, so either she or I could pick Jenny up at noon, depending on what worked out best for us.

As they drove off together, this time waving bye-bye to Daddy, I stood alone at the cabin door feeling as though my whole belly had been shot away with the sudden cannonball of missing them.

That's silly. Only half a day and they'd be back. I hadn't said much about it, but the idea of our little girl, barely a child, being dropped off at a day school with other orphans of today's life style just didn't sit right with me.

But I kept smiling and waving until they were around the first bend, into the trees and out of sight. Then, with a whole wonderful day to get all the work done I could, I just wanted to go upstairs, lie across the bed and cry.

Oh boy, it was quiet. Just a moment ago it had been pure

bedlam, Diane running her standard thirty minutes late, high heels hitting the floor, pursuing fleet-footed Jenny to finish dressing her and go through the ritual of combing and braiding Jenny's pigtails. Away they had gone, room to room, Diane shouting, Jenny shouting but always just one grab ahead in the race. At such times the most helpful thing I could offer was a civil silence.

Now all the hoo-hah had died down. I just stood there in the silence. Jenny gone to day school. Just a little bitty child, ours, who had never really been out in the world without holding on to either my hand or Diane's.

"All of this is for the best, Gordon," Diane had told me, and I had agreed. "Jenny needs some outside contact. She needs to be with children her own age." True. And it wouldn't hurt her any to be out from under the constant watchful eye of her mother a little bit either. All for the best. Sure.

C'mon Bax, let's sit down at the nice quiet typewriter with a clean sheet of paper, a calm cup of coffee, and gaze out over the creek and write something funny. I had found that I wrote my best comedy when my feelings were too strong to write the truth.

Jenny and Diane came home in the early afternoon, both of them just zinging with the excitement of the first day at school. Jenny babbled about all the kids she had met, all the great stuff in the playground and how much she liked her teacher. Diane was very pleased with herself and with Jenny, all of it shining in her eyes. I couldn't get much hugging done with Diane still wearing her office armor and being too restless to light anywhere. They both talked at once, paced around, their hard city shoes making a constant tattoo on the floor. Keats went and hid.

Day school was a great success. Jenny leaped into all of it, came home with stories of new friends, sang us new songs, and when Jenny was happy, Diane was happy.

I was still plagued with some moments of remorse, like

when they told us to laundry-mark all her garments. As I printed "Jenny Baxter" on her personal things I thought, institutionalized. My daughter is in an institution.

Sometimes Diane would call and ask if I could pick Jenny up at noon. The school was an attractive place. As attractive as any place can be behind a wire fence. The folks were nice. They would recognize me in the lobby and the receptionist would pick up her mike and page, "Jenny Baxter ... Jenny Baxter, please," the voice echoing in the hollow corridors of the prison back there.

Then around the corner and barreling down the long windowless hallway would come my own flesh and blood, Jenny, always at a dead run, pigtails aflying, face flushed with pure happiness and excitement. She never slowed down, I had to kneel and block her rush like a Cowboys lineman. Wham! Arms around me, kissing my cheek. "Dad-deeee!"

I was proud of her. Other kids, other parents watched this great scene. Some of those other kids came creeping out like possums into the daylight.

No prison to Jenny; she loved the place. All this bad stuff was going on only in my own head. I would watch her face when she saw the old pickup and realized I had come to get her and not Mom. In the old truck she would always ask, "Where's Mom?" Your mother's working in some office, your father doesn't have a real job, and you're behind a fence. Sorry, kid, that's just the way your life turned out. I never really said anything like that. These depressions never lasted long, but when they came they were bitter. Jenny would bring me back, trying to tell me something over the happy rattle of the old pickup. She was showing me a tear in her sleeve.

"How'd you get that?"

"We were playing." A happy grin.

Once she came home with a bite mark on her arm.

"A little boy bit me."

"And what did you do to the little boy?"

"I hit him." Utter satisfaction in her face.

And we would drive on home singing to each other.

CHAPTER 17

Leukemia Scare

Diane, rocketing in her new career, looked ten years younger. Jenny, boisterous with all her newly learned group-play games from school, was fast losing her baby look, becoming an uncommonly beautiful child. Her skin, so fair, was getting the first tiny sprinkling of freckles high on her cheeks, which seemed to go perfectly with her "dare me" disposition. Her hair was getting lighter as she grew older, a lighter shade of red than the color of new copper wire she was born with. She wore it in twin braids, or sometimes what Diane called "puppy-dog ears," just parted and pulled up above her ears on each side and held with a bow or a clip close to her head. Full of words, full of life, missing nothing, wanting to talk about it all.

When they left for work and school each morning now, I was content with my typewriter. The words were upon me.

Diane and Jenny came home late one day, and all I had to do was look at Diane's eyes to know that something was very wrong. I waited for a quiet moment and asked, "What's the matter?"

She sighed, looked away, and quietly said, "Jenny and I went for her checkup today. Her white-cell count is off again."

From the time of her birth Jenny had a slightly abnormal white-blood-cell count. She had regular appointments with our pediatrician, whose answer after each lab test was,

"Don't worry about it, come back in a few months." Today he had asked Diane to start coming back each week. "Benign neutropenia," he assured her, but Diane was plenty worried and a little mad too. She felt she was getting the pat-on-the-head and "There, there, little lady" treatment she detests. She was also concerned because traces of Jenny's ear infection had returned. Diane had gotten some new medication from the doctor but not nearly enough information to suit her. Where the average doctor misjudged Diane was in not realizing that she read medical journals and was probably as up-to-date on Jenny's age bracket as he was.

"I want to know!" she cried out in her anger and fear. There was one place she knew she could go and get all the information she was looking for. Diane packed her and Jenny's things and they were gone the next day to Dallas. To see Dr. Owen Coons. I didn't know enough about anything medical to know how scared to be. But I knew Diane and the folly of doing anything but giving her my love and support.

Dr. Coons is not a baby doctor. He is a flight surgeon with a background in the Royal Canadian Air Force and at NASA, and his practice is limited to air crew only. Diane had met Coons during her ten years of flying with Braniff out of Dallas. When I met Diane, I inherited Dr. Coons.

The flight surgeon is a very important figure in the life of any pilot, for without a current and valid medical certificate a pilot's license is worthless. It is therefore understandable that a pilot is less than calm when he makes his periodic stand before the flight surgeon. On my first occasion, he listened and lingered long with his instrument against my chest. At last I asked, "What doing, Doc?"

"Listening to your bloodstream."

"Can you do that?"

"Oh sure. And the blood makes different sounds as it courses through your plumbing, often giving an early clue to arterial troubles."

I waited as long as I could, then asked, "Well, how does mine sound?"

"Like the heart and vessels of an eighteen-year-old." Then

he looked straight into my face and broke into his beautiful smile. I've loved the man ever since, as much as Diane does, for his diagnostic skills and his application of these to the entire body and mind of each patient.

I was ignorant of whatever had sent Diane flying off to Dallas now, but I felt serene and comforted that she was going to see Coons. He, if anyone, could set her mind at ease. I relaxed as much as I could and waited for the phone to ring.

Diane called me that night from her mother's. Her voice was tight with control. Dr. Coons had been glad to see her, had bragged on Jenny, and the little girl had soldiered through all the lab work and tests without a whimper. They took blood. Diane had brought along her own previous notes and gave Coons a read-back which the doctor never doubted as being accurate. He knew Diane.

"The immediate report is that Jenny is pre-leukemic. He wants me to get her into Texas Children's Hospital here for a complete work-up. Right now. He helped make the arrangements."

Diane was giving me an official report. That's all. Simply giving me all the information I needed so that we could plan what next? Her control was saving her. Diane was never a screamer.

I made arrangements to fly to Dallas, and she met me in the terminal. Oh how glad Jenny was to see Daddy, shouting and hugging. I held her, staring past her to Diane. Our eyes met, full of fear and grief.

Jenny was so excited at having us all together at Granny's house, she wanted to run, play games. No, she was not about to eat all her supper, and no, why should she go to bed when all the rest of us were still sitting up?

We finally got her down long enough for her to quit fighting sleep and her eyes to drop shut, with me lying on the floor beside her cot. Once she woke, jerked awake and whimpered, and I whispered to her, "It's all right. Daddy's here." She reached a little hand down to mine, and went back to sleep holding on to me.

About midnight I woke up, found Diane sleeping on the

couch near us, all the lights still on and the TV too. A late-night disco. No sound, just the dancers, grimacing and twisting their bodies. I watched awhile, feeling our own horror deep in my chest. It looked like a scene from the *Inferno*. I decided this was what Baptists meant about dancing being a tool of Satan. At last I went back to sleep and my dreams of death, on the floor beside Jenny.

Staring into the darkness of my own mind I saw Jenny running in the sun, then imagined her tiny coffin. Where would we put her? Oh dear God, this ain't fair. Take me instead. Let Jenny live her life. Please.

Diane and I never had a moment to get near each other's feelings. It was probably just as well. I was there, her mother was there. All of us were extra polite and attentive in the little niceties like breakfast. We functioned. We held together and did what we had to do while on the edge of hysterics.

There seems to be some protective shield of numbness that comes over me at times like these. Like when my father died from injuries in the car wreck back in '68 and Mom died in the hospital a short time later. I never felt any all-out grief. It was just happening, that's all. I learned later that I never got through grieving for them. Their faces would come back clearly in my mind, laughing, faces of the good times. Diane would ask, "What are you thinking about, Gordon?" "Oh-h, nothing." What could I say? And so it went for me when awful things happened. My wall was strong. But it went on leaking forever.

I was beginning to feel the wall growing now. This could not happen to our Jenny, but it might. I was already experiencing it from behind that wall. It was awful.

Diane was fretting because the ear infection was getting worse and Jenny could take no antibiotics because of the pending blood work-up. The fretting and griping about details gave Diane and me something better to do than either talking or not talking.

I had to go back and do my weekend radio show before we knew about Jenny. "Hi, everybody, it's showtime!"

I did it. Did a happy show. But at the end I asked them to

pray with me. To send up a column of prayers. "I'll tell you what this is about someday when you are older." Then I just left the mike open and let the radio station hum to itself in silence. Not long, but long enough. At the end I said, "Amen." but I couldn't talk anymore after that. I played Mamma Maybelle Carter's "Wildwood Flower," my coming-in and going-out song. They know, my listeners do.

Diane called the next day. "Jenny's OK," she said. "I'm coming home."

She went on, "She had a bad infection in both ears. But the pediatrician was right about her blood cells. They told me that those same values in an adult would be cause to worry, but a condition such as hers is not too unusual for children. 'Go home,' they said. 'She's OK.' "

"I sure am thankful. Thank God. Come on home. I love you." There was nothing I could say that sounded natural or enough. Not for either one of us; both of us knew it.

I believe we prayed it away. I went out onto the sandbar and knelt down by an old stump at the edge of a willow grove beside the water. A big old water moccasin crawled out of that stump. I never moved. It just looked at me once, then slithered on into the creek, leaving S tracks in the wet sand and swam away.

I looked across the creek. To the forest wall over there and the summer cloud buildup in the blue sky. I had to keep telling myself it was over. That it was OK. I could come out now. I prayed, "Oh dear God, let us live. Let us grow old naturally in peace and love, please."

And then my mind wandered to a hundred years ago. The place would have looked much the same, and so would we, only we wouldn't have had all this laboratory science. We would have treated the earache with some remedy that Diane had learned from her mother and it would have gotten either better or worse. We would not have had this agony. We would have just lived or died, mysteriously. I wonder which was best. Well, God never changes. And we can't go back a hundred years either. I wrote at the typewriter all the rest of that day. Wrote comedy.

After they had come home and we had settled back into our life stream again I asked Diane what it was like at the hospital.

"I walked in there with Jenny so bright and full of life, and the first thing we saw was all those other children, sitting in their chairs so silent, with no hair because of their radiation treatments. Children in advanced stages of leukemia, sitting with their mothers. I was almost ashamed to be there parading Jenny in front of them. I will never forget their eyes following us. Nobody talked in there."

"What would you have done?" I asked. She knew what I meant.

"Whatever I had to do." My Diane.

She said the worst time was when they began to take Jenny's blood. One of the doctors' questions was, "Does she bleed easily?" Just then one of them put an otoscope into Jenny's ear and it began to spurt blood. "That's when I let go. I think it was the only time I cried. The bleeding was from her infected ear."

I never got past those days of thinking Jenny might have leukemia. Such a slender thread we all hang by. I never took risks again. None of the joys I used to know—a little wild flying or hurricane chasing. The high tempting of fate. No. I didn't begin to clutch at the passing of days, but a sober reflection of the value of life was born in me. Some wild innocence I had enjoyed all my life was gone forever.

Later Diane and I attempted to talk about this too, but got bogged down in the certainty of death that would eventually separate us. Diane quoted, " 'All of life is a process, and death is only part of that process.' "

"Well, you can't hardly ask for anything fairer than that," I wisecracked, and told her she was starting to sound Presbyterian.

"Better than trying to sound like an east-Texas redneck," she replied, and held out her arms.

CHAPTER 18

The Preacher
and the Bare

Rain clouds parted and a fresh watery light came down over the trees in their bright dresses of newly leafed green. Jenny and I kept this day to play. Just she and I; Diane was at work. Too many wet days, too many wet diapers, I let the nineteen-month-old Jenny run free outside in the rain, barefoot up to her shirt. We had just gone upstairs to put on a dry one when an unfamiliar little car drove up into the yard.

Jenny hunkered down by the big window, watching and wondering who this could be. Few people know we are back in the woods, fewer still can find us. Whoever it was, old noble dog Wolf was greeting him warmly, tail wagging. Yesterday our big shepherd had kept the electric-meter reader on top of his truck until I went down and properly introduced them. Deciding this must be a friend, I didn't hurry.

I squatted down by the window beside Jenny and saw two things. Our visitor was a stranger, a neatly combed man in a serious dark suit. I also saw what Jenny had done on the floor while squatting by the floor-to-ceiling open window.

"Don't move!" I shouted. The stranger in the yard down there froze. "Not you, I'm talking to my kid, you come on up." The confusion and panic had begun.

I sprinted across the room for a handful of paper towels and back again at the speed of light. Too late. Jenny was tracking it across the rug. The stranger was tapping on the door. Scooping up a laughing Jenny with one hand and as much of the rest of it as I could get with the other, I made it around the corner into the bathroom.

Jenny began to yell indignantly at having her behind hung over the washbasin and splashed with cold water. The stranger yelled friendly-like from the threshold of the living room, "Hi. I'm the Reverend David Holmes of the New Hope Baptist Church just up the road from you folks."

Oh lordy. A Baptist preacher, and me with a handful of . . . I searched my mind for some good clean Biblical phrase to cover what I had a handful of and why we were still in the bathroom. Finally I just yelled back around the corner, over the sound of Jenny's wailing, and told him. If he was any good as a Baptist preacher and was making his ministry in the creekbottoms of Hardin County, there was no use in coddling him now.

He was laughing when I came out of the bathroom with a towel-draped Jenny. He had settled himself into a little rocker right by the window.

I had another handful of paper towels. "Don't move, preacher, I'm using your shoe there as a marker."

I got the rug cleaned up with my rubbing and his pointing, all of us with our heads bowed together. Peace was restored. With a sigh I sat down facing him. Jenny leaned back against the window, regarding the man. She was at her most charming, her curly little head tipped to one side with a rosebud smile on her lips. The preacher began to talk. Then I noticed that Jenny had dropped her towel.

Ever see one of those classic cherub fountains in Paris or Rome? Know how the statues smile while filling up the pool? That's what Jenny did next, narrowly missing the minister's shoe.

By this time the preacher's embarrassment was starting to show. I just didn't give a hoot anymore.

"That's all the parlor tricks she knows, Reverend, except she usually sings for us, too," I said.

Jenny moved close beside me, turned up all those big bright lumens in her eyes, and we sang, "Jesus loves me, this I know . . ." with her clapping her hands in accompaniment.

The reverend, recovering well, allowed as how everything he had seen of her up to now indicated that she'd be a real good Baptist. Then he got serious and asked if we were doing anything early to let her meet Christ before the rest of the world got to her.

I thought of all our praying times. Just naturally praying. Holding hands and praying at mealtimes; out on the sandbar alone and praying. Some things that are natural in a man's life don't come out right when he has to talk about them. I told him I was a praying man.

I started to tell him this place is my sand-floored cathedral, but it sounded too hokey.

"Are you saved?" the preacher persisted. "If you died right this minute do you think you would go to heaven?"

"Preacher, I think I'd have to wash my feet for sure, and maybe they'd have to dip me again to satisfy some of those old naysayers who remember me from my old days, but yes, I think I would make it on across."

Then I asked the preacher if he would come outside on the porch and pray over us. We went out and knelt down on the open-front gallery overlooking the still beauty of the creek. While he spoke the words over us Jenny cruised along the pot plants that Diane has set out atop the wooden railing. Jenny found Diane's potting soil and eased up behind the preacher and offered him a handful of it. He looked warily, then breathed a sort of heavenly sigh of relief, spread his arms and went right on bringing the Spirit down on us.

He covered us pretty well, Jenny holding still now with her little head bowed. The preacher got a good roll going and went on, asking the Lord to take care of that new Sunday school bus he was needing, too.

He didn't stay too long after we went back inside the cabin; he sort of edged his way to the door, being careful of where he put his shoes, and invited us to come and visit at his church, soon. I really liked the man, promised we would. I thanked him for his ministry. So did my daughter, who had tested it pretty well.

CHAPTER 19

Power Struggle

Fair Jenny sat at the table in her high chair, a thundercloud scowl upon her brow, her red hair matted to her forehead, lips pooched out, her large blue eyes pale and roving. Our little Napoleon.

She had climbed the rungs and legs of her high chair, nonchalantly balancing high off the floor as she made her independent way to the seat. Now she was banging on her metal tray with the butt of her spoon. She wanted food. Now. And when her scurrying mother got it there Jenny refused to eat and scattered it across the room. This was Jenny at twenty-one months.

For a few awful moments, watching this display of tyranny, I realized I didn't like our child at all just then. Where was my chubby cherub who used to give me her little three-cornered-cat grin when she saw me coming and would hold out her little arms to me? What had happened so suddenly? Where had my little Jenny gone?

I reached for the book *The Second Twelve Months of Life*, by Frank and Theresa Caplan of the Princeton Center for Infancy and Early Childhood. If we were committed to a book-raised child, I needed the book, right now. I opened the book and it was all there: "The Twenty-first month. Power Struggle."

Jenny, it seems, was hammering her way out of being a

baby. She was able to open drawers, unlock doors and handle language, but none of it was quite working for her yet. She stumbled, she faltered, she raged. She would see a hand held out to help and she would yell, "No!" But as she yelled it she was reaching out for the hand. It was important for us to know when to hold, when to let go.

"Jenny, let's do one of your favorite things, let's go down on the sandbar and explore."

"No!"

As I reached out to lift her, she became a stone, suddenly somehow increasing her weight fivefold. I carried the stiff and yowling Jenny down the front steps and out to our place on the warm soft sands by the shallow creekfront. Jenny was yelling for her mamma. What her mamma needed right then was a little recess. My mind was thumbing through Caplan: "At this stage the child can grasp the concept of big things and little things and will copy you in simple work. Wants to help."

In the sun-warmed pools by the water's edge some freshwater clams were cut off from the main body of the creek by the dropping water level that day, and they were circling blindly, trying to find the creek.

"Jenny, look, there are big clams and little clams, they need help. They are trying to find their way to deeper water (just like you, my love). Let's help them."

Jenny and I sat down in the sands to work it out, together in the sun, cooled by soft May winds that rippled the surface of the creek. We picked up the clams and threw them back into the creek. Jenny pointed to our footprints in the sand. "Big . . . little," she said proudly. I pointed to the clams of various sizes. "Big . . . little," I confirmed. We looked at each other with the satisfaction of immense understanding. We had found something that worked for us.

A revived Diane came down the front steps of the cabin carrying two steaming cups of coffee. She settled herself on the bottom step. Jenny and I ran up the sandbar to her. Jenny wanted to touch her, too.

As we sipped our coffee and I told Diane the "big and little" story, Jenny backed off from us a ways. The ground slopes toward the creek here, made rough by tufts of grass, but Jenny, who is always careful of her body, kept her balance. She was looking at the little pathway that crosses in front of the cabin here and leads around the cabin corner and off mysteriously into the woods, out of our view.

Without saying anything to us, Jenny began to venture along the pathway toward the cabin corner. She stopped, stood there a long time, holding to the corner of the building. From the book I knew that in a moment she would turn loose and wander on up the pathway out of our sight. And that it was important we let her go. I looked again, Jenny was gone.

We could hear her faintly, back there in the woods, babbling and talking to herself among the tall tree trunks and the shadows and the wildflowers. Then suddenly Jenny was back! She came racing around the corner, looking anxiously to be sure we were still there, wanting to tell us all about it.

Jenny at her twenty-first month.

The bittersweet joy of letting her go.

In the wink of time we will be watching her going up schoolhouse steps to disappear inside. Then bye-bye, Daddy, as she proudly bicycles around some street corner completely on her own. Then the wave of a hand and out the door with some boy to his car. Bye-bye, Daddy. . . .

I looked up at Diane and found her watching me with the utmost tenderness, reading my mind again.

"You did good," she said.

CHAPTER 20

Murr Guze

In September of '79, with Jenny just two years old, Diane and I had another of those late-night, corner-of-the-kitchen-table family congress sessions. She asked what I thought of her going back to college.

She felt that she should have a degree in accounting for the work she was doing in the office. She wanted to be officially qualified in the event a job such as hers opened up in a place where she did not have the advantage of friendship to begin with. She mentioned the college credits already earned, that her college graduation was a goal she could achieve in just a few more years. She managed to get all that across to me without ever hinting at our twenty-year age difference and the likelihood that she will eventually need some means of self-support.

I listened carefully to her proposal: first the degree in accounting, then the exam for her own CPA license. When she was done, with no interruption from me, she paused, a silence asking what I thought.

I told her honestly that I liked all of it but was concerned about such a pace. Her job in the mornings, school in the afternoons, me and Jenny the rest of the time. Could she do all that?

Diane's only concern was an aspect I would never have thought of: "I don't want to look silly, a woman my age going back to school with all those kids."

I was a big help. I went into a fantasy of the tight jeans and loafers I would get for her, the beanie and the tight sweater, and told her I had always wanted to sleep with a coed. She said I had a one-track mind, and not a very good one at that.

The conversation having been switched, the decision to go back to school went almost unnoticed. So did Diane's return to the college campus. She came home laughing the first day to tell me of all the women her age who have gone back to school, "And nobody pays any attention to us." She was also delighted to find that some of the registrars remembered her from twenty years before, were glad to welcome her back, quickly rounded up her records and credits and announced that she was qualified to enter as a junior.

"It's campy to be a middle-aged woman on campus," she crowed. "Part of the revolution, you know."

I groaned and rolled my eyes, as was expected of me. I took on more time with Jenny, who was now in her genuine, certifiable "terrible twos." This was not much of a problem because I knew what to expect from her: "No." And I could still grin her into almost anything by making a game of it. I got the bedtime ceremony. A ceremony is a must because Jenny, like her mother, runs so hot and intense during the daytime that she needs gearing-down and unwinding at night.

The program began with bathtime. Jenny was a little pink seal in a brimful tub. She did not believe that anything above her shoulders needed soap and water. My problem was to get at the fine dirt necklace that all kids seem to be wearing by day's end. I would say, "Hopee-neck," which is what my mother used to say to me and which had gone from my memory until the moment I needed it. Jenny would then lift her ticklish little chin and I could do her neck and face if I was fast enough.

The signal that the bath was over was my saying, "Now you are a clean kid." She could climb out of the tub, stand glistening, waiting to be robed like a princess in a big fluffy towel. She would sweep grandly out of the bathroom, a trail of wet footprints leading to where Mommy sat over her studies. Here she got hugs and cuddles and was dried off all at one time. Then Diane would slip Jenny's little blue full-length nightie over her and I would pick her up in my arms for the "good-night waltz."

We sang it to the tune of "Sweet Betsy from Pike," and the words were different each night.

"Yer daddy sure loves you,
Yer mommy does, too,
So shut your big mouth
And your big eyes of blue.
You sure do feel good,
You smell like clean soap.
Dancing with you, kid,
Fills my soul with hope."

Thus we arrived at cribside, having waltzed into her room across a floor scattered with toys and coloring books. She did not want to turn loose, so the stuffed animals in her bed would begin to call her.

The blue elephant would say in a deep elephant voice, "Hell-oo, Jenny-poo, I sure have been lonesome for you." And a high funny voice would chime in, "Hi, Jenny, I'm your clown. Please come snuggle me so I can go to sleep." Then her favorite little doll would begin to cry in a little bitty doll voice. I would put Jenny down in the crib, pick up the doll, want to cradle it and tell it to hold on just a minute, Jenny would want to take the doll away from me. Reach for it, curl up and snuggle it, and in an instant her eyes were shut, her breathing deep and regular.

I would tiptoe out of the room and proudly present myself to Diane.

"She's down."

"She is?"

"Yup."

"Then who is that standing right behind you in the long blue nightie?"

Jenny and I would stare at each other. I think I would see a twinkle of victory playing around the corners of her innocent eyes.

"Now what?" I would ask.

"Murr Guze," Jenny would reply.

That is two-year-old talk for *Mother Goose.* She would point to the book on her own library shelf.

Jenny and I would hold hands while she lay in her crib and I sat on the floor reading to her in a soft and loving voice. The drone of my reading would soon put us both away for the night. When Diane had finished her studies she would find us there, me leaning against the crib, head in the book, Jenny sound asleep, too, holding my hand. Diane said we both snored but in different keys.

I would remove my hand carefully from my daughter's, she would stir and murmur, "Boo bah." That was leftover baby talk that she still used to ask for a bottle of milk.

"You already had your boo bah, now you are asleep," I would whisper.

Then Diane and I would stand and slip our arms about each other and look at her. We could still hardly believe the miracle of her. I would lay a hand on Jenny's warm brow, my heart spilling over. "Please, Lord, let her bed be always so warm and safe."

She was two already. Not a baby anymore. So fleeting the time for boo bah and Murr Guze.

CHAPTER 21

"Daddy always did have trouble with that."

Diane said, "The only reason you two get along so well is that you're the same age. Two and a half."

This is true. During our woods walks together in the forest freshness after a rain, I would let Jenny learn the proper use of mud puddles: to play in. We would start out being very careful and neat about it, then Jenny's foot would slip and with both arms pinwheeling she would sit, *ker-splosh*, into the water.

First the look of surprise at the cold water soaking in, then the look of anxiety at having fallen into the muddy water. Is this OK? Then, seeing that I was laughing, she would laugh, too, and reach up for a hand to help her out of the slick mud. From then on we both still tried to be as careful as possible, but after the first time what's a little more mud?

Sometimes Diane would see me and our little girl coming up the road from adventures such as this and threaten to just throw us both away. "Not necessary, we're wash and wear," I would assure her, and lead Jenny to the garden hose for the "You hose me, I hose you" which got us clean enough to come into the house.

Jenny and I had good fun and games, but there were still many times when she was just plain disobedient and defied both of us in some simple matter. Then my gut would churn at the frustration of not being able to do anything about it.

We were raising the child Diane's way, and that was that.

Even as I wondered if we were right in this business of raising a child who was not afraid of being hit, I looked for ways to persuade her to do what we wanted her to. Jenny would most often balk at the supper table. No, she was not going to eat her meat. Instead of getting mad about her not opening her mouth, I would make a little airplane of my hand and take off from her plate with a cargo of one bite of meat balanced on my fork. The meat flight would buzz overhead, Jenny watching, fascinated, then its engine would sputter and I would call Jenny on the plane's radio.

"Jenny from meat flight, Jenny from meat flight, open the hangar doors quick, we are out of gas and going down."

More engine sputtering, the meat flight circling, losing altitude, Jenny's eyes would be bright with the game, she would pop open her mouth, the meat flight would barely make it in. Saved again. And one bite of meat down. That was a good game, lasted us a long time with many variations. Sometimes she was pilot and I was the hangar doors. But sometimes Jenny would simply balk at anything we asked her to do. When I tried to put her little socks on she would make fists of her feet: "No." So I would pretend I was a farmer sacking pigs. A lot of jostling and shaking and grunting and squealing and snorting going on, but soon we had both laughing pigs sacked and ready for shoes. I was beginning to get the heady feeling that I could get Jenny to do anything just by making a game out of it.

But something else was on my mind. Though I still kept quiet about it, I was concerned about our daughter's cocky self-assured swagger through life. Sometimes I would grumble to Diane, "She thinks the world's her oyster. She shouldn't. It ain't. I'm not sure that raising this mostly disobedient child is a good service to her."

But Jenny was apparently not as self-assured as we thought. She began to stammer at day school, then at home.

She had been making very swift progress with words and loved to try out new and fancy ones. "That fascinates me," she would remark, proud of the multisyllable usage, and getting it right. The stammer crept in very quickly.

It was painful to see her try to talk. Nearly broke my heart to see her quick little mind trying to shove the block of speech impediment out of her mouth. I had to look the other way.

Diane and I knew to ignore it and made haste to the school to talk to her teachers. That was when we learned she had first begun stammering at school. They were a lot more relaxed about it than we were, assured us that they often saw stammering come and go among their little charges and that their policy was to ignore it, too.

Now we were worried about an element we could not control: would the other children ridicule her? Apparently not. At any given time there was at least one among them taken with the stammers.

With all the outside bases covered, Diane and I looked inward on ourselves, wondering what we had done wrong. Though we still had strong disagreements on child raising, there were no signs of this conflict that Jenny could tune in to. All she got was love and persuasion from a patient Mom and games from me. My arguments about obedience being essential to child raising took place across the pillow late at night.

One sparkling clear autumn afternoon I took Jenny to a children's playground. We were walking, her warm grip on two of my fingers reassuring to us both. A leaf spiraled down, and we stopped to watch such a remarkable thing although a million more might fall. I equated the falling of a leaf with the passing of the time she and I would have to share in our lives. The last of mine, the first of hers.

She picked up the red leaf and handed it to me and clearly and easily said, "Leaf." I took it and thanked her, not noticing just then that she had not stammered.

When she saw the swings ahead she turned loose of my hand and went barreling off toward them, head down, pigtails flying. This will be her approach to all of life, I thought.

The regular swing seats were about chest high to her. "Too high," she said. We found the low one.

"Push me, Daddy. Swing me."

"How high do you want to go?"

"To the sky, Daddy, to the sky!"

She swung to the sky, toes pointed, head back, laughing. "To the sky!" Not a trace of a stammer. I could hardly wait to get home, tell Diane, see if it was lasting.

The shadows were getting long. "Time to go see Mommy, you ready to go?"

"No." The usual answer. I thought how glad I would be when she was three and learned some other answer.

When we reached home Diane was hiding behind the door. "Boo!" A good gotcha. "Where did Daddy take you?"

"To the sky."

Jenny's face was still full of the beauty of it and flushed with excitement. Diane looked at me, tried to conceal her surprise. She had noticed immediately that Jenny's stammer was gone.

"Jenny, will you sing your ABC's for me?"

Jenny, always loving to perform, sang it all to her, ending with "X, Y, Z. Now tell me what you think of me." Diane grabbed her up, looked at me with the question in her eyes. I shrugged the "Don't ask me" reply. The stammer was gone. Gone as suddenly and as mysteriously as it had come.

Jenny was close to three years old, still obstinate and headstrong, but Diane's "learning to obey with love" was clearly working in many areas of her behavior. I conceded that after one day when Jenny and I went out to stroll the mall and look at toys. It was the first time I had a clear comparison of Jenny with other children. Children who had been raised the way I would have raised her.

We met a young fellow I knew who had his two little daughters with him, too. Beautiful little girls. One slightly older than Jenny, one younger. Jenny ran to them at once to make friends, talking, gesturing and telling them about the wonderful things we had seen. The two little girls just stood and listened. I was talking to their father, and when I introduced him to Jenny she looked up at him, smiling, and included him in the circle of conversation, not in any way intimidated by his being a grown-up.

I was watching the other little girls in contrast. Both clung to their father, shy and uncertain, as our little group stood in midstream of the shoppers in the mall. Jenny was asking them questions now, and they rolled their eyes up to their father as if asking permission to speak.

"You sure have a couple of well-behaved young ladies there," I said to my friend, secretly prying.

"They better be," he replied.

"How do you keep them so quiet and mannerly?" I asked, my question passing over the top of Jenny's attempt to make new friends.

"They just dad-gummed better be, ain't that right, kids?" he asked, hitching up his trousers meaningfully.

A thin veil of terror seemed to envelop the two little girls.

"You spank 'em if they need it, eh?" I pushed.

"Dern right. Never have any trouble with them. I sure am proud of these two." He spread his arms to lay a fatherly hand upon each of them. I would almost swear they flinched.

Meanwhile Jenny had given up on starting a friendship here and gone bombing off to the burbling indoor water fountain, hollering back at me for some pennies to pitch in.

"Well, I got a wild one, as you can see. Let me go take care of that now. Good to see you again." We shook hands. "And glad to meet both you young ladies." I offered a hand. They both drew back.

I went after the running Jenny, who by now had conned two little gray-headed ladies out of a penny, and the three of them were making a wish and bending over the fountain pool to watch the tossed coin waft down to the bottom.

I shuddered at my innermost thoughts as I joined them. I had been just like Billy Bob when I was a young daddy like him. And I was as proud of it as he was, too. "Yessir, my kids are well-behaved and polite. They better be." I had a quick flash of memory of how they sometimes looked up at me just the way those two little fawns had looked up at him. Never sure of when they would feel the power of Poppa's hand. I could hardly wait to get home again to tell all this to Diane.

Mine was an emotional confession that night. Diane hugged me to her breast, "When will you ever learn to listen to me?" she needled lightly, laughing. Then she made a confession of her own. "I was really concerned about our differences in child raising. I worried, so I decided to call your oldest daughter and ask her if obedience and discipline were all that important to you then. She's old enough to know and young enough to remember and has children of her own. And we like and trust each other. I can talk to her that way."

"Well what did she say? C'mon. Tell me." I was leaning forward, not to miss a word of this. All my life I have wondered what my children thought of me. "What did she say?"

Diane's eyes shone with love and humor. "All she said was, 'Daddy always did have trouble with that.'"

"That's all? That's all she had to say? A lifetime of having me as her daddy and all she had to say was that *I* had trouble with obedience?"

Diane was laughing now. "That's it, O mighty Captain, except to tell you that she loves you very much."

And so the three-year worry ended. Our Jenny, so open, so free, so confident, already the person she is going to be. This child of ours who doesn't even know that parents sometimes hit their children. For their own good, of course.

Texans are not supposed to cry, but I cry easily, try to cry silently. Diane had moved around to the back of my chair. She put both arms around me, rested her head on mine. "It's OK," she whispered. "It's OK. . . ."

CHAPTER 22

Love Is OK

Turn around, turn around, and she's a young girl, getting leggy, and now she was three.

Our schedule was demanding. Diane worked in the mornings, went to college in the afternoons. I worked at the radio station weekends and was trying to write. Jenny was just being Jenny.

"Talk to me, Daddy.... Read to me, Daddy.... Let's go outside and pretend we're motorcycles, *v-r-room v-r-room!* You can dress me now if you can catch me.... No. No. Let *me* do it. I'm a big girl now...."

She would pick up a pencil, hold the eraser to her lips and pretend it was a microphone and she was doing my radio show. "Don't be mad at me, Daddy, let's be happy. You smile with me."

"Jenny, I've got to write." How could I tell her I had something else I was supposed to be doing when here she was a brand-new person wanting to try it all out on me? When the publisher called from New York and wanted to know where the copy was, how could I tell him I was playing with a kid?

"Let's go out and walk in the dark, Dad."

"The gravel hurt your feet, hon?"

"Yes."

"Want me to carry you awhile?"

"Don't worry about it."

Oh, the good old days when I just carried her.

We had to celebrate each full moon. We would go outside and find a clearing in the trees so she and I could see it. I would hold her up in my arms and we would sing, "I see the moon, the moon sees me . . ." I didn't want to miss any of it. Then we would find the first star and she would sing, "Starlight, star bright . . ."

Jenny loved to perform for us. For everyone. She could now count to twenty in English and to five in Spanish. Her grandfather taught her that. She could recite the alphabet or sing it, she knew the Pledge of Allegiance and all the words to "You Are My Sunshine." We still sang together when rattling and clapping along in my old pickup, Bluebelle.

Picking a book out of her library and having her mother read to her at night was a very special time for both of them. They would curl up on the long couch together, their hair gleaming under the soft light, and I would look upon them with my heart full of love and pride.

"Are you going to kick and scream when I put you to bed tonight?" I would ask at last.

"Oh, a little. Mother, are you frus-ter-rated?" She loved new long words, assembled them carefully in speech.

She wanted to know all things. "Why do things fall down instead of up?" "What does 'happen' mean?"

She quickly adopted the telephone for her own use. Diane made up a little card file for Jenny with the numbers she called most, printed big and bold. Jenny would race us for the ringing phone, putting a lot of breath into answering, "Hi-ii-i . . ."

At first I worried about her answering the phone. I hate to have to parlay my way through some bratty kid to get to the person I am calling. But Jenny was crisp and courteous. Or maybe I just think that because it was my kid on the phone.

I did hear her take a call for her mother one day while Diane was napping. "My mother is not feeling well just now. But I have a surprise for you. I've got a reindeer, right here on the table."

She passed through quick phases. One day her mother came back from college eager to get her arms around Jenny, but Jenny was not at the door. She was sitting at one end of the couch, cool and composed. She patted the cushion beside her. "Sit down here, Diane," she said.

Diane was shocked. "I'm your mommy," she corrected.

"Yes, but inside you are Diane. You have to be Diane."

That experiment lasted a couple of days and like to have broken her mother's heart. "I'm gone too much," Diane whispered to me, looking windblown and frightened.

The time of the great questioning went on.

"Why is water wet?"

"Because it's liquid," said Diane.

"What is liquid?"

"You can't hold it in your hands."

I was admiring the answers as much as the questions. Then: "How did I get in your tummy, Mom?"

Diane told her about the seed, the ovum being fertilized by sperm from Dad and the creation of life within. Jenny was studying her feet through all this. "I think my toenail polish has died," was her only comment.

Then about two days later came the one I had been waiting for. We were driving home in the dark, a favorite time for Jenny's mind to range far with questions. We had been talking of all sorts of things, and now a comfortable silence had come. Diane and I were lightly holding hands, when from the back seat Jenny asked, "But how did Dad get his sperm inside your tummy?"

Oh boy, I thought, how will Diane handle this one? I admit to tensing up at the wheel, staring out into the night, stealing side glances at Diane to see how she was. Composed.

I was glad Jenny had asked her mom. My answers too often are in wordy essay form. Diane answered in simple direct words. "He put his penis inside my vagina," she said.

That was all. That simple. I let out a long sigh of relief.

Later Diane and I talked about the wisdom of using proper language with a child in describing sexual organs and personal functions. The words sounded cold and clinical at first, but Diane was never a "wee-wee," "too-too" mother. "Urine" and "bowels" said it fine.

I came to be grateful for this. Jenny, our unabashed daughter, had the words to discuss whatever part of her body she needed to. She felt no false shame in herself. She could come to her mother and accurately say, "My vagina is irritated and burns when I urinate." And she could get the same prompt care as she would for a skinned knee.

I asked Diane if she had gotten such straight sex answers from her own mother when she was a little girl. "No." And I was curious to know how far this blackout of sex talk had extended. So was Diane. She asked her sisters if any of them had ever had any sex education. No, they hadn't. Then we asked her mother if *she* had learned anything from Grandmother? "No." And at last we went to Grandmother, tall, dignified and beautiful at age ninety-one. Had she been told anything about sex by her mother? "Of course not."

So it went. She told her daughters nothing, they told their daughters nothing. All the way from the nineteenth century to now. All good Christian women.

But there was one area where Diane was as strict and proper as her Victorian ancestors would have been. That was in the monitoring of what Jenny could see on TV. Jenny was not allowed to fill her little head with the daily bill of fare of shootings, stabbings, chokings and beatings that most children are exposed to if left unattended with the set.

Diane simply told Jenny directly, "We don't watch any shows where people are hurting each other." And we didn't.

So Jenny learned that she could ask all she wanted to about loving, that love is OK, but hurting people is nasty.

CHAPTER 23

The Optimist Club

I should have imitated Diane's straight answers to Jenny on any question. But no, I had to go and make a comedy of things, with results sometimes unforeseeable and regrettable.

At the table one night: "Jenny, drink your milk."

Jenny back to me, "I don't want to drink my milk."

"Drink your milk," I said, "it will make hair grow on your chest. See?" And I pulled up my tee shirt and bared my chest to her.

"Aw, Dad, you're fooling me. *Men* have hair on their chests. Women have breasts."

Diane shot me the Warning Glance about giving Jenny funny examples.

A few nights later, we were enjoying the great treat of eating out at the Dairy Queen. As we sat in our booth, two little old ladies recognized me. They smiled in a friendly manner and one of them leaned over from their adjoining booth and said, "And this must be Jenny whom we hear so much about from Daddy on the radio."

Jenny sat quietly through this exchange of pleasantries. Then she noticed that the little old ladies had not touched the glasses of milk set before them.

"You better drink your milk," said Jenny.

I thought, Oh-oh! But it was too late now. I tried to vanish in my booth. Events marched quickly on.

Like bright birds, the two turned again and focused on Jenny. "Drink our milk? Oh, tell us why, you darling little child."

"Because it will make hair grow on your chest. See?" Jenny was standing up in her seat now, pulling up her blouse, pointing to her chest.

The two little old ladies were speechless. Jenny sat down, laughing, looking to me for applause. Head in hands, I thought of Diane's favorite expression for times like these, "Omigod. Omigod." The smart kick in the ankle from Diane was not really necessary. I had already learned my lesson.

The ladies turned to the privacy of their own booth and to their supper. I looked down at my sweetly smiling daughter. You will never convince me that this little person, here among us for less than forty moons, not only had mouse-trapped dear old Dad, but knew it.

One might think I had learned permanently from this, but oh, no. Only a few months later Jenny came home from school and shot me the finger. Instead of a speech on such vulgarity I decided to show her a much older traditional American hand gesture from a more gentle and humorous time. I told her she would be the first kid in her class to know this and she could do it to anyone who made a vulgar hand gesture to her. I showed her how to thumb her nose. And how to do it with both hands if she meant it to go double.

Diane said softly, "You'll be sor-ree."

Oh, she was right.

A few nights later I was the invited speaker at the local Optimist Club. It was Wives' Night, and we brought Jenny too. We had no baby-sitter; Jenny likes people, enjoys the crowd, and we enjoy having her along. We basked in all the reflected glory she attracted that night. We took our seats at the head table, I as speaker seated next to the speaker's podium and the club president, Diane and Jenny to my left. When they introduced the head table Diane stood up, bowed, promptly sat down. Next they introduced our darling daughter. She was beautifully done up in a white dress with ruffles at the shoulder and along the hem, and her hair was one long shiny braid. She looked so good. Both of my ladies did.

Jenny responded to her introduction by standing up in her chair, placing her thumb to her nose, and carefully panning the group so as not to miss anyone—she double-thumbed her nose at them all. Little cherubic fingers waggling, her face so solemn and serious. Some of the old "Yanks" from World War I when the gesture was popular began to cheer and applaud. The others took it up, not being sure of what else to do. Diane, beside me, gave a distinct low sound that only I could hear. Her Momma Lion growl.

It was to be a long night for Jenny, just sitting at her place, eating in a ladylike manner. She lasted well into the time when the speechifying began. But when they got around to introducing me and I started to stand up, I noticed from the corner of my eye that Jenny was gone.

It could have happened at any time, like when I was making table talk and leaning away from her. Now her chair was empty. It was my turn to growl. I knew what she was going to do. Another game Daddy had taught her.

We called the game "Submarine." Another name is "Guess who." It involves making your way under the surface of the table tweaking folks. This was going to be awful.

Few noticed the little girl submerge beneath the white polar cap of the table tops, but as I looked out over the rows of well-fed Optimist and their wives it was easy for me to keep track of my daughter's subtable progress. There would be a sudden jump from one person, a startled look, followed by an accusing glare at the person seated beside them. Jenny would surface at the end of the table row, give me a victorious little wave and a grin, shuttle over, submerge and start back down the next row.

What a great time she must be having. Tables much longer than our kitchen table where she got her training, rows and rows of unsuspecting legs. I could just imagine her under there. It was all I could do to not crack up when I stood to begin my speech. I don't have any idea what I said to the Optimist and their wives that night. Sometimes I would look down to hide the grin and I would see Diane's fists in her lap, slowly clenching and unclenching.

Jenny got clean away with it. Was standing by the door looking innocent and doll-like when the meeting was over and they all headed out. When our eyes met she and I were both grinning and trying hard not to bust. Later Diane warned me again not to teach Jenny anything in private I was not ready to go public with. But it's like I told the good folks of the Optimist Club, I don't think I ever enjoyed a meeting as much as that one.

CHAPTER 24

Playing Rock

In November of 1980, Jenny age three years and three months, Diane called a kitchen-table congress to give me her reasons for quitting college. "Jenny will be four, our last two years of her at home before she starts public school. I'm missing too much of it." She rounded out the fall semester at the university and retired for a while with honors. She had made a perfect 4.0 average in advanced accounting.

Jenny and I rejoiced at having Mommy on hand once more, and we presented to her a brass-on-wood wall trophy with her name, the date and that 4.0 on it, thus setting out Mom's academic record for posterity.

With Diane at home more and us more relaxed, I tried to show in small ways how much we appreciated her. On Sundays I always made the run down to the mailbox and brought back the paper and served it with coffee in bed. This time I decided to try breakfast too. Jenny wanted to help. Standing on a kitchen chair beside the stove, she offered to do the eggs. She began to tap an egg on the edge of the skillet.

"Are you going to break that egg or just wear it out?"

"I'm breaking it, Dad—oops, there it goes, right through my fingers. Oh, that's yuchchy!"

"It's OK. Try the others. Oh-oh, same thing, eh? Well, I'll tell you what, let's scramble them. You know how to scramble eggs, don't you?"

"No, Dad, I thought you did."

I was trying to scramble busted eggs in a hot skillet. She said, "That sure is a mess. I think Mom scrambles them in a bowl first."

"Well, it's too late now. Don't tell your mom about this and we'll feed them to her anyhow. Moms eat anything."

Jenny bent over the stove. "That's looking worse and worse. Smells bad too."

"Maybe we could put some chili in there. Boy, look what that's doing to the skillet," I mused.

From the bedroom I could hear Diane softly laughing, like the Biblical Sarah in the tent. I had thought she was still asleep.

"Go tell your mother breakfast's ready."

"I don't think she's going to eat this. And I won't."

"Let me put lots of salt and pepper on it. That's what seasoning was invented for, to cover up crimes in the kitchen."

Diane joined us in her robe, looking all soft and rested, full of ill-concealed mirth. "How are the eggs?" she asked, knowing very well how the eggs were.

"Well, different."

"Dad, I can't eat that stuff, and I don't think Mom will, either."

"Picky picky, all of you," I said. "Here, I'll try them out on the cat." I quickly opened the kitchen door. "Kitty, kitty . . ." My tomcat Keats ran up, stopped, sniffed, backed away.

"Come on, you wretched faithless cat. Think of all the times I've taken you to the vet, your head almost torn off from some Saturday-night folly. You better not betray me now."

Keats looked apologetic, stepped aside.

"How you doing?" Diane called from the kitchen table.

"Not too good," I admitted. "I think Keats is trying to cover them up."

These were gentle times on the creekbank with me, Diane and the kid. In the soft language of the South "kid" is not contemptible, as it sometimes is in other parts of the country, but rather a diminutive term of affection. A young cowboy on the plains, the new boy with an oil field crew, will be called "the kid" if they like him and he shows promise. "Kid" even becomes a term of endearment between lovers, ranking along with "honey" in use and meaning. Parents saying "the kid" are expressing great affection in our part of the country. Our kid was constantly growing and testing her progress and ideas on us. She needed someone to bounce new ideas off of all day long.

At the allergy clinic, waiting for a regular checkup, the kid was in outstanding form. To a lady patient who was trying to read a magazine she said, "I haven't picked my nose since I was three and a half years old."

"How old are you now? asked the lady, the whole roomful listening.

"Three and a half," said Jenny with a grin.

Contests of will at bedtime became louder and longer now. One night Diane told Jenny she must lie down and go to sleep and no, she could not get up and get any more toys out of her toy box.

"Oh yes I will," shouted this child raised of love and reason.

"You will get spankings. Many spankings," threatened Diane, now pushed across the line.

"How many?" asked Jenny, the power passing to her now. "How many? Three? Will you cut my ear off?"

I stayed out of these confrontations, even stayed out of the room to avoid becoming a third-party reactor to either one of them. But once in a while when things escalated to the shouting stage I would step in swiftly, gather up the yelling kid close in my arms, take her out into the cool of the night and walk with her along the edge of the sandbar even as I had done when she was just an infant. The rhythm of my walking, my song, the stars and the moon would quickly calm our little storm trooper down.

When Diane and I talked about this later, she said that what worried her most was the look of fright that seemed to come into our daughter's eyes when her rebellion carried her past the point where she herself had any control. Diane said the security of my hugging her close was important to Jenny.

"Brat," I muttered to myself. Not for the record.

Instead of flashing at me as I expected, Diane spoke in a soft voice. "No. She's trying out a lot of things. The limits of control, who she is going to be. She has to have someone to try it all out on, to learn what works, what doesn't."

Some of the places Jenny went through during this time of passing from babyhood to childhood are haunting for me to remember, even now.

Once she woke up in the night, calling fearfully for her mother. We both ran to her bed. She clung fearfully to her mother, sobbing. Was she sick or having a first nightmare?

"I don't know where I am," Jenny sobbed.

"Where do you think you are?" asked Diane, holding the child close.

"In a dark place . . ." was the answer I can't forget.

On other nights we would hear Jenny singing; singing alone in the dark. We would go and stand beside her little bed. She said she was singing to a star. A star named Billy Jones.

"What does the star do?" I would ask gently.

"Oh, he just flies around and shines down on the earth that God made," came her calm cheerful voice.

These episodes worried me. Out of some primal memory of my own, I related deeply to Jenny's waking alone and afraid in the night or even waking to sing a solitary song in the dark.

Diane assured me that she believed it was all a part of baby Jenny's passing into childhood and not something we were doing wrong with her.

"I wonder why she still resists bedtime so mightily," I said.

"Two reasons, I think," said Diane. "Haven't you ever felt as though a great day was ending too soon? Haven't you ever felt that way when a day was just going great for you? And the other reason is just as strong. She is so much a part of what we do all day long that it's hard for her to understand why she's the one who has to go to bed while we're still up and having fun."

I nodded, thinking how lucky both Jenny and I are to have a person like Diane.

But Diane has her limits, too. One night she was anxious to just settle down with a new book and do some of what she called "throw my head away reading." She had settled into her favorite chair with a cup of hot coffee, and Jenny settled right beside her, ready to play with Mom.

"How does God make hair?" asked Jenny.

"I'll ask God," mumbled a preoccupied Diane.

"Do it now," Jenny persisted.

"I will next time I say my prayers," said Diane, still trying to read.

"Listen, God, Mom's going to ask you a question." Jenny was pushing her.

Diane turned to me with a look of despair. "Play a game with her. Any game, please. A quiet game. Just give me ten minutes off duty. That's all. Ten minutes."

I told Jenny to come with me, that we had a brand-new game. She was beside me in a flash, wanting to know all about it.

I told Jenny that this was a very quiet game, being quiet was the whole secret of it, and we needed the old quilt that was on the floor in the hall closet. Jenny was right back, dragging the quilt.

I began to speak in hushed tones. I told her we were going to play rock. That I was going to play it first so she could watch and understand. I crouched under the quilt, completely covered up, in the knee-to-chest position, my arms wrapped around me, and I didn't move or make a sound.

Soon Jenny came creeping in under the quilt and imitated my humped-up position and silence. After a time she broke the silence by whispering in the dark, "What are we doing?"

"Playing rock. Big rock and little rock."

There was a long thoughtful silence. Just we two rocks.

"What do rocks think about, Dad?"

"They think about the earth," I whispered back. "Rocks are very close to the earth."

"Oh."

More absolute stillness. I felt half guilty for getting away with this so easily.

"I think I'm sweating," whispered Little Rock.

"Rocks don't sweat. That's why they last for such a long long time."

"Are rocks old?" asked Little Rock.

"Yes. Very, very old. We are too heavy to move and not good to eat or make soup out of, so people leave us where we are."

"Oh."

More long silences. I drifted pleasantly in and out of sleep. I was beginning to believe we might be just two rocks.

"What are you thinking about?" whispered Little Rock, keeping perfectly still.

"I'm thinking about God. God put us here, didn't he?"

More long silence. At last Diane couldn't stand it any longer, looking at the absolutely still and silent quilt on the floor with the two lumps under it.

"What are you two doing now?" she asked.

I decided not to answer. People are always trying to get answers out of stones. But Jenny replied for both of us. She murmured from under the dark quilt, "We're just a couple of rocks, listening to God."

CHAPTER 25

Mantelpiece Picture

Diane's family reunion in Dallas for Christmas of 1980 brought the culmination of a longtime crisis created in my own imagination. For years I had felt threatened by Diane's mother. Not that she ever did anything hostile toward me; she was always loving and smiling. That's what bothered me. Diane loves her mother so much, Jenny loves Diane so much. I always felt like just an old rooster in the yard, tolerated by the hens. They were on the phone to each other a lot. Jenny was excited at the prospect of Christmas with Granmaw, Diane was excited at the prospect of seeing her mamma and dear old mam-maw, her own granmaw. I felt like a temporary spur in the whole matriarchal ma-ma, gran-ma, mam-maw, world of theirs.

Last summer when Granmaw and Mam-maw came down to visit us at the creek I lined them all up to get a good picture of all four generations of these women. Not just four generations, but three centuries of them. Mam-maw, her name was Pearl, was born in 1890. She was a mature young woman when the men marched off to France in World War I. She had light-red hair, same color as Jenny's, worn in a braid like Jenny's too. The slender old lady was ninety-one, and when she smiled at you she smiled with her own teeth. Most of the time she lived alone in the little rock-hard town of

Cleburne, Texas, south of Fort Worth, and made her own way in life sewing for the public. There was a great dignity about the woman. Old Mam-maw had come to Texas in a covered wagon. There are still many of these women pioneers left. They may well be indestructible. But hardly any of the men survived.

Diane's mother, Sally, still a handsome and feisty blonde of my age, riveted B-24 bombers together at Consolidated near Dallas during World War II. Diane was a war baby, her dad a South Pacific Marine, Mam-maw helping to raise her. And, last, Jenny, born in 1977, will be only twenty-three when the next century begins.

What came into focus in my mind as I photographed them all was how temporary and passing my own role might be on this earth.

All these feelings came back to me during the Christmas visit to Dallas. The house was full of sisters, aunts, great-aunts, nieces, mammas, daughters and lots of granddaughters, but hardly any men. The men were represented by a grayed photograph, carefully framed and set on the mantel. They were wearing their best suits, nonsmiling.

I got the horrors. What picture of me, in what suit, would Diane select to set on the mantel after I was gone? I made a resolution to myself that when we got back to Beaumont I would go see old friend and photographer Wayne Baker, and tell him I needed a mantelpiece picture. He'd understand.

Diane's dad, Rogers, a quiet brilliant man, was there. Self-made, an independent geologist, he had a worldwide reputation for finding oil and a family reputation for not getting any of the money. He seemed as miserable as I, even in his own home, but more experienced at it.

Jenny loved her grandpa, flew to his arms when we got to Dallas. He had taught Jenny to count in Spanish. On our visits to Dallas, Rogers would find quiet times to be with Jenny and teach Spanish to her. That was their game. Rogers, although fair and blue-eyed, was drawn to all things Spanish. He had taught himself the language years ago by reading and by lis-

tening to the Mexican radio stations one can hear all over
Texas. In Mexico his love was returned. They called him "the
blue-eyed *amigo*."

Rogers would cast a mischievous eye upon me standing
against the wall in that room full of welcoming women. He
knew my mind. He also used my predicament to needle his
wife. It was an old game.

Sally was serving coffee in her fine china, and he called,
"Come on back in the kitchen, Gordon, and let's you and me
have some *real* coffee." I would follow, he would set out his
battered percolator that had seen Lord knows how many oil
field camps, and brew up coffee you could drink or slice.

Back in the parlor a short time later, he would say to me in
a low voice that nobody missed, "Let's go on into my room so
we can talk some sense."

All the women would keep on talking at once and smiling
at each other. Sally would just smile sweetly at him. I would
follow him out, feeling that I had been compromised into
casting my lot, and with the losing side at that.

During this holiday visit, with everyone gone shopping I
found myself alone in the house and hungry. My mind else-
where, I drifted into the kitchen, got the bread, the peanut
butter, then the jelly. I was taking a knife out of the drawer
when I had this awful dawning: Good grief! How could I have
known where all this stuff was in my mother-in-law's kitchen?
I hadn't hunted for anything. I went right to it.

Sandwich in hand, but appetite dying, I realized that I
knew where it all was because it was exactly like our house.

I hurried to the bathroom to see if I could find the clean
towels at first try. I did. Same with the cabinets where Sally
kept the home remedies. Same home remedies too, same
brands. Exactly like our house, all of it.

"I haven't got a chance," I moaned softly as I collapsed on
the long couch, set in the living room about where Diane
would have set it. "This goes all the way into their bloodstream. Someday Jenny will have a house laid out just the way
this one is."

I went on with the pitifuls. No real need for me, a man, being here. I had already done all I was needed for. From here on I was just a hanger-on.

Diane knew something was the matter the minute she got back. Mentally she sniffed me over. "What is it?"

"I'll try to tell you later," I said, not wanting to start a Class-A fight here and spoil Christmas at Grandmaw's.

When we got back to the creek and I tried to tell it, Diane was quiet, thoughtful; studying me, but quiet. Clearly she was going to let me work it out by myself. All she said was, "You do know how much Mother loves you, don't you?" She meant her mother.

I went on feeling sorry for myself. Then one day, putting the bright pictures we had taken at Christmastime into our family album, I began to see those four women in a different way. I began to see the beauty of their closeness and their love for each other. To see how unique and fortunate they were. I envied them briefly, then the thought came: the only thing keeping me out of all this was me. It was that simple:

I began to try to find ways of making friends with them all. No problems with Jenny, she and I were the same skin. Always had been. With Diane it was mostly to be less critical of her. Her own words came back to me: "People can be different without one being wrong."

With her mother and her mother's mother I couldn't rush in and shout, "Hey! I decided to love you." Not with them unaware I had ever felt estranged, for there was no reason apparent to them why I should be.

One problem, small as it seems, was in not knowing what to call my mother-in-law. The "Mom" or "Mother" I had tried at first sounded hokey and it was. So I just began to call her by her name, Sally. That was a big help to us both.

Then I began to look for happy-hands work around her house whenever we were in Dallas. This would give me something to do that would also tell her more than I could with words. Rogers, who was not and never had been a Mr. Fix-it, showed no resentment. He did, however, understand what was going on. We all did, and loved each other for it. Whenever we got to Dallas and all the shouting and hugging with Jenny died down some, I would just ask her what jobs she had saved for me. I ended up keeping a small set of tools at her house.

With the grand old lady, I asked Diane how we could show our love for her. Diane was writing to her grandmother at the time. She did not reply in words, but took a crisp twenty from her wallet and put it into the letter, looking up at me meaningfully. I nodded.

Grandmother wrote to us in a fine Spencerian hand, her brief letters always ending with the same into-eternity phrase. "—Always remember how much I love you," signed "Grandmother."

Only once after we began to send money to her in our letters did this dignified woman ever come near to acknowledging what we were doing. She wrote, "Gordon, your special letters mean a lot to me." I later learned that her social security had somehow gotten mixed up, she received little or none of the money due her and was too proud to "go down there and beg for it."

Life was easier for all of us on the trips to Dallas after I grew up enough to recognize love. But it is still spooky to be one of the last remaining males. The long line of men in my family had shuffled on out to the end of the board until now I was the oldest, standing out there with my toes over the edge. The tradition amongst Baxter men was to live fast, die young and leave a beautiful memory. "Ashes to ashes, dust to dust, if the liquor don't get you then the women must": a family folk song, whose singers are all gone now.

I decided to change the script for this one Baxter. Young Diane and Jenny—so much love I wouldn't want to miss. But just in case the mantelpiece picture turned out real good: "That was Dad in his best year, near sixty."

CHAPTER 26

Understanding Death

August 26, 1981. Our Jenny was a child of four, proportioned like a miniature woman, getting picky about what she would wear and becoming very proud of her long hair. Brushed out free, Jenny's hair was a light-red flame to the center of her back. Diane had never cut it.

Jenny's hair is fine, tangles easily. Diane would unbraid it, brush it out, part it and braid it back each morning. To hear this ritual each morning, you would think Diane was taking out Jenny's toenails with pliers.

She tried various shampoos and hair conditioners, tried all the models of hair dryers, electric brushes, and dryer-brush combinations. Nothing helped.

"If you don't stop howling and twisting away from me, I'm going to cut it. That's all. I'm just going to cut it."

"Oh no you won't. It's too beautiful," said Jenny, who rarely suffers from lack of confidence.

I tried to help. While taking Jenny to school I would explain that she needed to be more cooperative when Mom was helping her.

"But she hurts me," Jenny sulked.

So one morning I pointed to a pair of those flat neat little cardboard boxes that long tapered candles come in. They were on the dashboard of the truck. I explained to Jenny with a very solemn face that if she continued to play uproar at hair-brushing time each morning I was going to present her precious braids to her, laid out flat in those very boxes, to keep as a lifelong souvenir. I could feel Jenny sizing me up, looking at the side of my face as we hammered along in the old pickup through the freshness of the day. I just looked straight ahead; stern Daddy. Jenny decided not to risk anything smarty. She let her little hand creep into mine and was quiet.

Some women, I tell you, are born knowing.

When Jenny was four Diane decided she would attend a dancing school. Not tap or ballet, just a typical little girl's dancing school, run by "Miss Bonnie," who is loved and remembered by generations of little girls now with children of their own. The beautiful Miss Bonnie never aged, and ran her school on USMC Camp Lejune boot-camp principles. Just a look from Miss Bonnie would silence the ranks.

We attended our first parents' night, the children all in black leotards, showing off beginner skills. Most of them were leggy, wispy, transparent as mayflies hovering. They circled before us. That's when I first noticed that Jenny was more compactly built. Not chunky, she was never anything but trim muscle, but, as I whispered to Diane, "Butterfly she ain't."

My wife did not think this as amusing as I thought she would. "I know she's not a butterfly. She is not built like a dancer. She is here to learn graces and to be with little girls her own age."

It was shortly after the little recital that Diane served two cups of coffee at midnight and called a kitchen congress to order. I thought she wanted to talk about our solid butterfly but I had guessed wrong.

"I have decided to quit the accounting office. What do you think of that?"

I waited.

"I enjoyed being a working wife and found out I was good at something. I can always go back to work and I plan to at some future time, but right now we are looking at the last two years of Jenny as all ours."

I nodded, agreeing.

"In no time she will be six," Diane continued, speaking low into her coffee cup, "then into school, then eighteen and off to college, then gone from us forever. I'm leaving the job as soon as I train someone else to run the office."

I thought of Diane in the office, how much she enjoyed it. I would often drop by and have coffee with them. In June I gave Diane a surprise birthday party there. She turned forty and I hired a clown to come in and give her forty black balloons. There are times when my idea of wit runs counterproductive to my own basic well-being. I wouldn't have done it if Diane looked a minute over thirty, everybody knows that. Don't they?

Diane's transition from working wife to housewife was as uneventful as her deciding to go to work in the first place. Jenny and I quickly used up whatever leisure time she may have thought she would gain. But she did look more content. She was easier on herself and on us with no bells to answer.

Then within two weeks we got the news from Dallas that Diane's grandmother, Pearl, was dying of cancer. Two weeks later came the call that told us her father was, too.

The grief in Diane's face went deep. She spoke little of how she felt, but showed all of it. She began to call her mother each night; we made trips to Dallas. The family drew in upon itself.

Rogers left the hospital to stay in his own room in the back of his home. Sally's mother was put into the front bedroom. Sally took on a role that was heroic, losing her mother and her husband at the same time in the same house. It was a grim time, but no one felt any way except that home was the best place to be.

Stoically dying, the grand old lady said, "It's all right. I have lived a long, long time. Longer than most. I am ready to go and meet the Lord." But Sally said she sometimes heard her crying in the night. Her cancer was abdominal.

Rogers was silent. His cancer was in his throat. His way of handling his fast-approaching death was to ask Sally to give him a party. To invite all his lifelong friends and oil field cronies. She did, and he sat among them in his robe, weak and wan, writing replies to their jokes on his notepad. For this was the way of such men in facing death.

A last letter that Rogers cherished was from one man who wrote back afterward, "Only you would arrange your own wake while you could still sit up and enjoy it."

We were much in Dallas at the end. "I am working my way through the process of grief," Diane told me. And I watched to see how she would handle all this with Jenny.

"What do we tell the child?" I asked.

"The same thing we tell each other," said Diane.

Diane simply told Jenny that Mam-maw and Grandpa were going to die. This set Jenny to worrying about her own death. And the cat Keats's and our old dog Wolf's. And ours.

Diane's answer was to explain carefully to Jenny that people die from one of three reasons. Some from accidents, but we are very careful: we used seat belts and had a child's seat in the car for her; we looked and listened before crossing the streets in town; and we have strict rules about not playing on the creekfront alone. Some people die of disease, but we were healthy and ate foods that were good for us, and we took care of our bodies. And some people die when they are very old, worn out.

Jenny came back to this several times, asking how old various people in her life were. Oddly, she never focused on how old I am. And I didn't bring it up.

Diane had to admit to our little one that we will all die in time, but for Jenny, she said, it would be a long, long time. "You will be an old woman with grandchildren of your own. That is difficult for a little girl to imagine, especially one for whom having to wait an hour before she can go out and play seems an eternity."

Jenny made a cross of Tinker Toys and told Diane it was to put beside Grandpa's bed so that when he died God could come and nail his spirit to it.

She also asked if it would be OK to ask God to tell Grandpa "Hi" for her.

"That would be a very good thing to do," said Diane.

During our trips to Dallas in the last days Diane would explain to Jenny about her Grandpa having no voice and about all the medicine bottles and things in Mam-maw's room. We always gave her the choice of whether or not to visit with them. In those last few weeks if we missed Jenny we would find her sitting beside her grandpa, patting his arm and telling him stories. And she wanted to help take the tray of food into Mam-maw's room and eat with her.

On the night when we got the call about Rogers' death, Jenny could see us in our grief. She went into the bathroom, she got the cleansing powder out of the bathroom closet and, standing on her little wooden tooth-brushing stool, she scrubbed out the lavatory. "It was something to help," she said.

We explained funerals to Jenny and gave her the choice of going or not. At her grandfather's funeral she was unsettled only once and that was when they served Communion. She couldn't see why she had to sit in her pew alone while everyone else got up for Communion. Neither could I. And so, with none of the usual church sanctions or ceremony, Jenny took First Communion.

Coming out of the church Jenny winked at some of the folks sitting in the back. Just by way of being friendly.

Six days after Rogers' death, we got the call announcing Mam-maw's going. In the days afterward, Jenny would sometimes say wistfully how much she missed them. How she wished they didn't have to die. "We too," was our only honest answer. Jenny was more concerned about us than with any deep grief of her own. She loved them, but they were not a part of her everyday life, yet her mind was open to the strong currents passing among us. She was groping to understand it all, knew it was tragic and important, but the child was not stricken with sorrow except in the passing moments of the events. For this we were thankful.

Diane had her own way of working through her grief. She did not leave her grandmother's gravesite when the funeral director tried to herd them all back into their cars. She stood out there in the heat by that mound of Texas limestone and red dirt and watched the backhoe come up. She stayed and listened as the tractor operator scooped up the first load, heard the dirt and stones hit the coffin top.

I stood aside, left her alone. In my mind I will long remember her like that—the little figure in black, her dress blowing in the ceaseless prairie winds, standing alone while the earth received the remains of the old woman who had held her as a baby, had opened books to her on the carpet beside her tall glass-fronted bookcase.

Diane stayed with her own thoughts in the wind and the reddening Texas sky until the new-made grave was mounded over and patted down by that skilled backhoe operator who also seemed to understand her aloneness and her need to be there.

At last it was done, and I came and took her arm and walked her back to the car. She was steady and dry-eyed. "I had to experience it all," was all she ever said.

One night back home Jenny found her mother alone in the kitchen in silent tears. She put her little arm around Diane and said, "A Frito and a hug will make you feel a lot better." Diane's eyes were smiling again as she came in to tell me about it.

Rogers' death had a surprising and lasting effect upon me. I guess I identified with him more than I knew. He was only a few years older than I; both of us were fair-haired men of light build, both of us competent free-lancers in our own fields. With his death I was now the oldest surviving male in either family, his or mine.

Now I had his beautiful daughter. Somewhere, someday, some younger man will have mine. I hope he will relate to me in the easy way Rogers and I related to each other. We seldom talked about Diane. It was as if Diane was a statement so strong that nothing else needed to be said.

We took Rogers back to his hometown of Milford, south of Fort Worth, out where west Texas begins. Here there is only a skimpy covering of topsoil over the stark-white limestone. They had to blow open his grave with dynamite. We agreed Rogers would have liked that.

But I still think of this man so alive, now encased in limestone so still.

CHAPTER 27

"Who takes care of me?"

Jenny at four was thoughtful. "Dad, how does God make people?"

"He makes them out of Play-Doh, lays them all out on a cookie sheet, then puts them in the oven a little while. Then He takes them out and pokes them with his finger to see if they're done." With that I poked her in the navel, said, "You're done."

She giggled, twisted away. "Dad, you're fooling me."

I told her I certainly was, then we had some running, chasing and poking. We needed to find games again.

We played hide-and-seek, which was easy enough with Jenny if you just waited long enough and listened to where the giggles were coming from. But one time the house stayed quiet. Too quiet for too long. I began to get a little scared in my seeking, my mind still too full of how suddenly families can be separated. I did some serious looking and found her curled up in the clothes dryer.

After the fatherly lecture on the dangers of playing in the clothes dryer, Diane asked her in a more loving tone why she was in the dryer.

"Because I needed a place to think."

"You could go to your room and think. It's a whole lot safer."

From the dryer Jenny replied with words that still haunt me, "I know. But I needed a round dark place to think in."

Jenny, our Jenny. What manner of delightful, mysterious woman-child do we have here? I decided we needed to get out of the house. To make an expedition of some kind. Soon.

"How would you all like to drive down to the beach?"

"Oh boy, oh boy, how soon? Now, right now?"

Now was the time Jenny lived in. It took some explaining that now was bedtime and it was getting dark but we would go to the beach tomorrow. She was up early.

I was excited about it, too, taking my daughter to see her first ocean. The beach of the Gulf of Mexico is only fifty miles due south of our woods-wilderness home. We went in the afternoon, the beach road through the salt-grass prairie taking us to the oceanside at last. There it lay in the afternoon sun, the Gulf of Mexico, flat and shimmering, beyond the last low sand dunes, reaching out forever. How can one tell of the limitless ancient sea to a four-year-old?

There is no way, just give it all to her freely. I lifted her and held her up in my arms to see and felt her shiver with excitement. We took off our shoes and ran to the sea. A race to the edge of a continent.

She stopped at the low curling surf. "Is it deep?" Good. Her creekbank training.

"Not at first. The first part by the sand is shallow and made for playing and racing, but on out there it's deeper than you would ever believe. C'mon, let's run!"

We raced along the ocean's edge on hard-packed wet sand, splashing through the tails of waves as they came ashore from far away.

"Taste it," I said. We were standing now, catching our breath, Jenny gazing in wonder at the water which had no other side.

She bent and scooped up a handful to her lips, spit it out. "Yuccchy-y. It's soapy."

"No, that's salt. The whole ocean is salty like that."

"Who did it?"

"God did. He made the ocean salty just like he made the sun and moon and stars."

She was standing in the surf, a ninth wave rolled in, higher than the others, caught her, soaked her. She backed off, holding her arms out away from her sides, her face full of surprise and not liking being wet. She looked at me to see if this was something to laugh about or not. We both laughed.

Then we ran along the seaside again. Ran shouting back to where Diane was walking along slowly, head down, looking for the perfect shell. I sent Jenny to her with a ghastly fish head we found bobbing in the surf.

"Omigod! Put that thing down! Where did you get that? Oh, you and your father!" Diane was backing off, Jenny and I were dancing around her, flapping the fish head. "Throw that thing back!" commanded Diane. We did. "What are you doing, Mom?" Jenny was now watching Diane's shell hunt. Diane told her, and she was instantly beside her mom, head down, hands clasped behind her back, moving slowly in the measured pace of the shell hunter. Jenny did best at it, too, probably because at her height her eyes were much closer to the shells than Diane's.

"Where is this place, Mom?"

"It's called the Gulf of Mexico."

"Is it big? Bigger than Beaumont?"

"Much bigger. It goes all the way out to South America."

Jenny stood, windblown, looking far out to sea, trying to think of all these things.

Too soon there was a flaming sunset and the wind grew chill. Another foot race was the only way to get her back to the car.

"I'm wet."

"We know," said Diane.

"My feet are all sandy."

"Sit here," said Diane, motioning toward the car door sill. Then she got out the dry towel. Someday a study should be done on mothers always having a dry towel.

We rode along in silence, darkness coming, Jenny nodding

off in the back seat. "First ocean," I said to Diane. She squeezed my hand. She knew.

We drove along in contented silence on the nearly deserted beach road. Then I heard Jenny shifting forward in her seat. I had thought she was asleep.

"Daddy . . . who takes care of me?"

The question, the hidden fears I read into the echoes of it, brought a dozen answers to my mind at once. I tried Diane's direct style of answering. I said, "Your mother and daddy do."

But no, I couldn't just leave it alone. Not with Jenny a captive audience here and us with miles yet to go. I began on matters of faith. Went into a lengthy description of how God, our Creator, cares for us while still giving us the free will to choose good or bad. That God loves us.

No comment from Jenny. So I went on into the care from the family. From Grandma and Aunt Sue and her godparents, Betty Em and Bernardo. From this theme I gave an enchanting little talk on how family life is so important and how fragile these relationships are, and how threatened by our rootless ways in America.

The car rolled through the night. Jenny sat in silence. We neared home and I went into my wrap-up, a grand summation. I told her how her mother and I, God and His angels, her family and her godparents all had an interest in taking care of her.

It was about as good a presentation as I ever made. All forty miles of it. Now we were turning into our own driveway. I was silent, waiting, hoping to hear some response from Jenny.

At last her voice came from the back seat.

"That's nifty," she said.

CHAPTER 28

Faramont School

In September of 1981 there was a small ad in the Beaumont *Enterprise*. It was notice of the founding of Faramont, a small private school for gifted children. Testing was open for children four or older.

"Do you think she's a gifted child?" asked Diane.

"I don't know, but I would sure hate for her to find out we were even considering such an idea," I replied.

We met with the school and agreed to have her tested. We also agreed that the term "gifted child" was too loaded for household use and adopted the phrase "exceptional child," which Diane had read in a magazine article.

"Gifted child" doesn't mean that Jenny could sit at a piano for the first time and play Chopin to perfection. Today's more common meaning is that she is bright. Quick. Not concentrated on any one "gift," but with an advanced overall understanding of things and an intense curiosity about all things.

In a few days, Monty Sontag, Ph.D, co-founder of Faramont School, called us in to see him, told us we'd better sit down, gave his graying Vandyke a few strokes, and announced with obvious relish that Jenny had tested out in the 99.9 percentile on the national level.

"I sure don't envy you folks," he said gently.

We asked almost in unison what he meant by that.

"You'll find out," was his only reply.

That night Diane asked how I felt about our Jenny being an exceptional child. What did I think of her going to Faramont?

"It was luck. Pure luck. This late-in-life child of ours has been blessed with the best berries off the gene bushes from both sides of our family." Diane agreed.

"Now I'm safe at last," I added.

"What do you mean?" asked Diane.

"Someone to take care of me in my fast approaching dotage. With my mind and your ambition Jenny is sure to become the first woman President of the U.S.A., and then I can lean back and become the darlin' of the White House press corps. On light news days they can just write about President Jenny's old man . . ." I trailed off, laughing, enjoying the image.

"You'd really do that, wouldn't you?"

"Ya betcha britches, yer dern tootin—heh heh heh."

"O.K., you can save all that, you're not out on the porch of the White House yet."

The two years Jenny spent at Faramont were fruitful and a pleasure to us all. She quickly began to read and write and do simple arithmetic. She loved the work, loved coming home to show it to us. Faramont and its tutors became an extension of our family. Those two years passed quickly, ending when Jenny completed all that the school had to offer and prepared to enter public school.

Her days at Faramont ended with considerable excitement. The national organization of schools for gifted children was holding its annual convention in New Orleans, and the founders of Faramont were invited to come and share with the others their experience of opening a new school, and to bring along a sample. They invited Jenny.

Oh, I was proud. I had visions of Jenny in the Temple, instructing the Rabbis. We talked nothing but smart to her for two weeks in advance. I thought mothers got wound up about their little darlin's appearing on the stage. I was silly.

On the fateful day of her appearance before the forum

Jenny stood on a table so that all could see and hear her. Before all those elders and scholars, she smiled, she twisted her braid, picked her nose, and gave them monosyllabic answers.

"What do you like to do?"

"Play."

"What do you like to play?"

"Batman."

I groaned. I gave up on the whispered coaching and just sat back and studied our child. I noticed that either her freckles were getting bigger or she was getting very pale. I asked, "Jenny, would you like to come down?"

"I sure would." I lifted her off the table in my arms.

Oddly enough, although they had seen little of the real Jenny, they crowded around her, loved her, exchanged addresses with Diane and gave the impression that it had all gone very well. Maybe it had and Jenny's dad had simply not been smart enough to see how.

After fleeing the room, I asked Jenny what she would like to do next. As her reward. Her choice. She said she would like to ride that elevator.

The hotel was one of those new styles with a lobby that rose from floor to roof. This vast hall was served by a glass-walled elevator adorned with gaudy lights. The elevator rose and fell like a tethered rocket, most of its occupants cringing back as far as possible from the terrifying view.

Jenny had the glass wall all to herself, enjoying the fake greenery, ponds and waterfalls dropping away with the speed of a bullet, then rushing back up at us again as we dropped out of the sky. Jenny chortling, cheering the whole great show.

I wished some of the professors had been with us then. Gifted, wifted, this kid has great zest for life.

CHAPTER 29

From the Woods

Schoolgirl Jenny went through the fives so quickly. She was happy, so was Diane, but there was a steadily increasing pressure on me from both of them to move off the creek and into town.

There was school, and dancing lessons, Jenny had joined the Bluebirds, and Diane seemed always on the go for one reason or another. She didn't push or shove about needing to live in town, she pointed out small things like the two round trips a day she sometimes made adding up to eighty miles.

Jenny was more direct. "Dad, I need people," she said, gesturing across the solitude of the sunlit creek to the utter silence of the forest wall beyond. "There's nobody here for me to play with."

My agony was in wanting to be the good father and provider and yet everything about this place that was ideal for me, the recluse, the writer, was wrong for my family. How I loved the creek cabin. I had designed and built it with my own hands and blood. I knew every board in it by its Christian name. Village Creek was in the marrow of my bones. My peace began when I turned off the stinking hot freeway and disappeared into the cool freshness of the hidden tunnel of trees that led back to my place on the creek.

Diane solved it by taking matters into her own hands. One

day she and Jenny moved out. Loaded the truck and went to town. She moved into a little house we had bought a short time before with the idea of renting it out. Not big or impressive, in an old but good part of Beaumont. Back streets with old trees that met over the middle, a neighborhood mostly of older couples. We never got to rent it. My wife and daughter moved into it and left me to my solitary musings on the creekbank.

That lasted three days and three nights.

I sulked. Let 'em go. Who cares? That woman moved right out from under my roof. It was peaceful now. Oh lordy, was it peaceful. I was dying of the peacefuls.

I found myself going down to the water's edge to find Jenny's last footprints in the sand. I left Diane's coffee cup untouched where she had put it down on the corner of the kitchen table when our last negotiations fell apart.

On the third night I rang the doorbell at "Diane's house" in town, carrying only my toothbrush. The door opened, they both stood there framed in warm light.

"Dad-deeeee!"

It was over.

I left the creek in miserable increments over a period of about a year. The first plan was to spend the nights with my family and work daytimes at the creek. A reverse of the town-house idea. Now it was me commuting. Sure used up a lot of my day.

The second plan was to rent the creek cabin to one of my sons who loves the place. Our agreement was that I would keep my desk and typewriter in one corner of the glass room and call before I came up. As the tenant he could redecorate and change the walls and furniture to suit his needs.

Nothing could have prepared me for the shock of seeing our home the first day he proudly put all his stuff in place and on the walls and stacked ours in what was once Jenny's room. I went out on to the sandbar and walked and wept alone.

"Diane, you'll know I'm really gone from there when I move my typewriter back into town." I was surprised at how soon I did that too. I just didn't want to see the place anymore.

One last idea: Maybe Jenny would want to come back if she and I took a gentle day and went up there just to visit and play. We walked along the road holding hands. "This is the road I used to walk and sing to you at night when you were a little bitty baby and your tummy hurt."

"Uh huh."

"We used to cut right through the woods here and backpack all the way to the mailbox. Would you like to do that again someday?"

She wasn't listening.

Inside the cabin I said, "And this used to be your room."

She looked at the new-made storeroom without comment or memory. We went down and played in the sand awhile, built a sand castle, then: "Dad. I'm ready to go home."

Home. Oh my love, home. I carried you up those steps when you first saw light of day. Home. OK, home. We drove Bluebelle, that good ol' pickup, back to Beaumont, making up goofy songs just the way we always did.

Her mind drifted off to *Dumbo*, which we had seen last night on the Disney channel we could now get since we lived in town. "Dad, when the movie opened, what were all those birds carrying in bundles on their beaks?"

"Those were storks, delivering babies."

"Delivering them from what?"

Then she watched me with candid pleasure as she does when she knows she's gotten off a good one but does not exactly understand why. Everybody knows where babies come from. What's so funny about that?

Jenny found people in Beaumont. Found friends before we did. She just walked over next door and said, "Hi. I'm Jenny Baxter."

Dorothy and Wilbur Balmer, a gentle retired couple, were sitting out in their front yard in lawn chairs, enjoying the cool of the evening. Watching sharp-winged martins diving at the birdhouse Wilbur had built in the front yard. Enjoying their flowers and tomatoes growing. An American flag stood out from the front of their house as always. They had lost a son-in-law in Vietnam. That kind of people, the Balmers.

"Well, hello, red-on-the-head," said Wilbur, and thus began an unusual friendship between our five-year-old and the folks next door. Not really a grandparents–grandchild relationship. The Balmers have grandchildren of their own. This was a genuine liking between Jenny and the "Boomards," as she called them.

We need not have worried that Jenny would make a pest of herself over there. When Dorothy had enough of Jenny she just sent her home. But there were also times when Dorothy came over and asked if Jenny could come play.

A fine friendship developed between Diane and the Balmers, then spread to include me. I began to experience neighbors again.

I noticed in time that I began to say "our house" instead of "Diane's house." And there really were a lot of conveniences to living close to the stores instead of planning a provisions trip into civilization now and then. But on nights when the moon was full I would go outside and stand in our cement driveway among houses and try to remember how the moon looked reflected in the creek when the only night sound was the booming of hoot owls instead of the constant freeway sound from just a few blocks away.

On one such night the neighborhood was ripped by a youth bent over the handlebars of his four-cylinder Japanese motorcycle, screaming through the gears. As my head turned, watching him go by, I met the eyes of old "Boomard," standing out at the end of his driveway too.

Each of us could clearly read the other's mind.

"Wouldn't want it to kill him," said my neighbor.

"No, just eat him alive."

We turned back toward our houses, chuckling at the moment of spontaneous rapport.

The Balmers began to baby-sit for us, another city advantage we had done without. Such an occasion was always parlayed to include Jenny's opinion. "You want to sit through an hour or so of speeches or stay with Dorothy?" I think this is what lawyers call "leading the witness."

Diane was extra careful to not lean on Dorothy, and we learned that Dorothy never played games with words. "If I don't want to, I'll tell you so," she said. Such people are comfortable to be around.

The Balmers were helpful in another, more delicate area. While Diane had not raised Jenny to believe that Mom and Dad never had any arguments, she would sometimes send Jenny over to see Dorothy if one looked as though it might escalate into stuff we didn't want Jenny to hear much of yet.

Just such a buildup was taking place in the kitchen one evening when we felt Jenny tapping both of us on the arm. We stopped, stared at her.

"You folks better calm down," said Jenny. "The Balmers are not at home."

CHAPTER 30

Smarty Pants

Jenny foraged for kids in the new neighborhood and found them, made new friends at school too. There were slumber parties, mammas bringing children to play with Jenny, we crossing town to some address where Jenny would be welcomed by a schoolmate for the afternoon. We often had a shy little girl or two underfoot and found long afternoons of peace and quiet if Jenny had someone to play with. Great castles of imagination were built, little dolls talked, both real dolls and toy dolls. Diane let Jenny and her friends have the run of the house for whatever they needed. I would sometimes come home and find all the sofa cushions stood on end, used as building blocks, and little-girl faces peeking out from their wonderful secret worlds.

I liked having the kids around, all but one little brother who announced in a loud clear voice as he and his sister were standing in the doorway waiting to go home, "Jenny's daddy is an old man."

I was not as mature about this remark as I should have been. "Scat!" I yelled at him. "Get outa here!" He scatted.

Sorry at once, I looked at Jenny to see if I had hurt her feelings. In the manner of her mother she was covering the laughter in her face with both hands. Nobody liked the little brother much, anyhow. He came with the sister, a sort of package deal.

I also wondered, with a little unspoken fear, if having real kids to play with now would bring an end to the closeness between my daughter and me. I needn't have.

"Come play with me, Dad?" Or the surefire way of getting me to stop writing, "Are you too busy to play with me, Dad?" That one always brought memories of love lost when I was a young dad and was too busy to play with the children of my first family.

Sometimes I would try to put her off. "We played all day today. Didn't I take you with me in the truck, we sang songs, visited in stores, wasn't that enough?"

"I mean really play with me, like blocks or Leggos or something. Just taking me with you was not playing with me while you were talking to other people."

A lawyer, I decided. She will grow up and become a Philadelphia lawyer.

A favorite game was "Announce me," in which I played my natural role as the announcer and she was a star. We had a sawed-off-broomstick microphone for this. "Ladie-ee-s and gentlemen, from the worldwide world of spoofs, tonight we proudly present Miss Jenny Tittle Baxter, the ravishing redhead from Redwood, who is about to . . ." The act depended on what she had last seen on TV. Wonder Woman in a long cape, or Spider Man, or her old friend Batman. Jenny with eyes shining like searchlights would do death-defying leaps off the back of a heavy living-room chair, cape flying.

At other times it was the six-o'clock news, and she took the mike. "Good evening, it's time for the news," she would intone, rising up from behind the chair. "For the immediate Beaumont area we are reporting rain, floods, thunder and lightning, wrecks and robberies and a stick just fell across your power line and put out all your lights. Good night." And with that she would slowly and dramatically sink off the screen.

Jenny often had the sniffles, some vestige of her allergy, Diane said. Her mother would interrupt a game and say, "Jenny, go blow your nose. That looks awful."

"I know," she would say.

"Jenny!" I would intercede.

She would turn to me and say in an aside, "I'm grossing Mom out."

"Jenny, blow your nose," Diane would call again, and Jenny once turned to face her and just blew her nose. No Kleenex. And stared at her mom.

"Jenny," I said in quiet disgust, "you're acting like a baby."

"I'm not a baby, I'm a child."

"Sometimes I have my suspicions about that too," I grumbled.

Jenny, at six, had started to ask me more complex questions and then before I could finish the answer she would interrupt with "Oh, I already know all that," when she didn't.

I went to Diane to discuss this new smarty trend. "Do you think it's my using her in that TV commercial we produced last week? She was good and easy to work with, but while we were on location she said, 'I want to be the star.' I told her we already had a star. Me. And she said, 'Just wait and see.' "

Diane heard me out, then reached way back for one of her philosophical replies. "The greatness of this age is that she has not yet learned to say 'I can't.' Look at her paintings. Could you be that bold with a brush and color? Her mind is limitless right now. Only later will she start to learn limitations and to restrict her own self-concept of what she can do and what she can say."

I thought all that through and saw the beauty of it. "But nobody likes a smarty-pants kid very much."

"She must have upstaged you pretty bad on the TV commercial," said Diane, being no help at all.

Another trendy name for Jenny's conduct is "free child." Jenny and I used a little of that on Diane one day and found the limits of Diane's philosophical replies. In the oral history of our family it has become known as the Episode of the Black Dress.

I had been asked to emcee a black-tie affair. I asked if I

could bring Diane and Jenny. Diane said, "I'll need a new dress. A long one."

"What about the dress you got married in?"

Diane gave me a pained look.

We set aside an afternoon on the mall, a whole afternoon of dress shopping. Jenny and I were to be seen, not heard.

At the first fancy-dress store, all they had were those pastel-colored, funeral-home dresses. I told her she looked good in black. To go for a black. She found a rack of blacks, but none full length.

"These are two hundred and fifty dollars," said the saleslady.

"For *one?*" I shouted.

Diane stepped on my foot. We left.

In another store we found a full-length black, a low-cut job that I really wanted to see her in. "I don't really go for these drop-dead necklines," said Diane, but she went to try it on.

While she was in the booth I whispered to Jenny, "When your mommy comes out in that dress let's me and you both drop dead. Cry out, clutch your throat, fall to the rug, roll over and kick your heels in the air just like I do."

Jenny thought this was a great idea.

Diane swept out in the low-cut black, we both shouted, "Oh wow!" and dropped dead. We drew a pretty good crowd too.

We didn't stay long in that store either.

In the last fancy-dress store Diane found a real Southern-belle black formal. Fitted bodice, v neck, all ruffles at hem and shoulders.

"Buy it," I urged. "Hang the cost."

"But I feel like a tart," protested Diane.

"A little of that wouldn't do you any harm," I replied, then quickly recognized such talk as nonproductive.

Jenny and I made solemn pledges to behave, and Diane tried on and bought the Scarlet O'Hara. She was still worried about wearing it for the first time to a formal, so I suggested we wait until Jenny went to sleep, then I would chase her around the house in it a few times until she got used to it.

"Listen. If you want me to go. To wear this dress. Then you better button your lip about it now."

I did. She was beautiful.

We had been concerned that the Faramont experience would place Jenny out of synch with the public-school system, and that worry was justified. As a first-grader she would come home, fling her Crayolas aside and look for a good book. "How'd it go at school today?" I would ask.

"Kid stuff," was Jenny's reply.

From some teachers there was a faint air of antagonism and jealousy toward the Faramont kids who were entering the system. The attitude was, "All right, if you are so bright, then show me." Children only six years old were unable to understand this pressure.

But Jenny was lucky to get a mature and dedicated woman as a homeroom teacher. She was above the pettiness and was curious about Jenny's capabilities and limitations. She counseled us on the problem of Jenny "fitting in." "She is such a free spirt," said this beloved teacher with masterful diplomacy when she talked to us.

In many small ways Jenny and I kept our close link as she expanded her world into public school. She came to me for advice about boys.

"Dad, there's a cute boy at school that I really like. Why does he always shove me?"

"Daughter, watch him and his other friends who are boys. They shove each other. Shoving is the only way a six-year-old boy has of showing that he really likes you."

"That's crazy."

I agreed, thinking of the really crazier days she had yet to see.

Jenny still went barefoot a lot at home and was forever limping in with a "sticker" in her little foot. I kept an official Splinter Kit. It contained a ten-power jeweler's loupe for seeing a vivid close-up of what was stuck in her foot and the best way to approach getting it out; a fine needle used to lift the splinter or piece of glass or whatever; and some very fine tweezers, bought at a medic-supply house, for the extraction. No blind digging around. She called me "Dr. Toe " for such operations and my payment was that she had to sing "The Song." Jenny would sing:

> *"From a broken heart*
> *To a diamond ring,*
> *Daddy fixes everything."*

The song was also payment in full for repaired dolls, shoe straps, rocking-horse bridles, record players. We are both going to keep on believing the song for as long as possible. Maybe forever.

The child Jenny had a new going-to-bed routine. "Snuggle with me," she would ask of one of us. And this was the time when either she would read to us or we would read to her. Oh she was proud of her new skill at reading.

Although I would have been just as happy to go back to Mother Goose, Jenny was caught up in the stories from a children's Bible. I enjoyed this too, in fact found it to be the only times the Bible made much sense to me.

We were in the Old Testament again, having read the Good Book through and through a time or two. A shadow crossed Jenny's brow one night as I read to her of the deaths of Abraham, Isaac and Joseph, those old patriarchs.

"Daddy, are you afraid to die?" she asked simply.

My answer was slow coming; the words I was saying were a profession of faith. "No, not much. We are all children of God. He promised us here in this book that we would all meet again in heaven."

"Can I bring my toys?"

That got her mind off me. And I tried to explain to her the lack of need for earthly things in heaven. She interrupted. "If I can't bring my toys, then I ain't going."

The old Jenny again.

Sometimes we played Bible games mixed into daytime fun. With her blocks and Leggos we built the walls of Jericho. Tall and wavering walls in the middle of the living-room floor. We marched around them in the role of the Israelites six times, blowing imaginary rams' horns. On our "seventh day" we marched around the walls of Jericho seven times, "When I say 'Shout!' we will both shout," I told her.

We stopped and shouted together, loud as we could. To our utter amazement the walls of Jericho swayed, then all fell!

Jenny and I stopped and stared at each other, not sure of what to do next. We tried it again on other days, but the walls never fell for us again. But Joshua remains one of Jenny's favorite people from the Bible.

Jenny began a campaign to get Diane and me to stop smoking.

"It's bad for your health and it smells bad to me. Why don't you both stop it?" asked our woman-child.

Putting my guilty old pipe out of sight, I tried to explain. "Our smoking is a habit."

"What's a habit?"

Try explaining that to a clear-minded six-year-old while keeping up the sham that it is you the adult speaking.

She wouldn't eat at a table if there was an ashtray on it. Who could blame her? We honored her wishes.

Then she raised the pressure one Sunday morning in our favorite after-church restaurant. "Are you two going to smoke?" she asked.

We assured her we were just dying for a smoke.

Without another word Jenny marched off to the no-smoking section and seated herself there, picking up the menu.

In a short time the waitress came over to our table and asked, "Is she for real?"

Feeling rotten and guilty enough already, I tried a little humor. "Yes, take her order, but get cash. Her checks are no good."

There was hollow laughter. The waitress left, Diane and I lit up. Tobacco never tasted worse. "Smarty pants," I groused.

"No, a human individual," Diane corrected. A fine line in the bringing up of children. Jenny had pancakes and sausages and milk. Ate them alone at her table.

CHAPTER 31

We Kept the Braid

I didn't think we would ever cut Jenny's hair. The red braid, waist length, had become a part of her. She was unconsciously expert at flipping it over one shoulder or the other, keeping it out of her way. She absentmindedly toyed with the end of it when she was thinking of something else. In school she was "that kid with the long braid." Finding her in the crowd of children when we came to get her after school was easy. Just a matter of looking for the light-red head, the long braid. If her hair ever bothered Jenny, she never mentioned it to us, even though she had to move the braid on one side of the pillow, because it was too thick to sleep on.

But the morning yow-yow between Jenny and her mother went on, had become a tradition to start the day with. Jenny yelling at pulls and snags, Diane threatening to cut it all off. Neither of them listening much anymore.

Her hair was beautiful worn full down, but so fine that the slightest breeze would tangle it hopelessly. Jenny never wore her hair down and free. She couldn't. There was too much of it.

In the summer of her "six-and-three-quarters" year, as Jenny called it, she and her mother began to talk seriously about cutting the braid.

The reason was their plan to let Jenny attend a Bluebird–Campfire Girls summer camp. At Camp Niwana, deep in the backwoods, she would have no one to braid her hair each morning, and she couldn't do it herself. The braid was Jenny's only dependency on Mamma and home.

I stayed out of it.

Both my ladies were trying to be considerate of my liking her long hair. Diane wasn't going to get off free, either. The night before their appointment at the beauty shop Diane whispered to me across her pillow, "This is her last dependency on me."

When I was certain we were going through with it there was a flurry of picture taking. I got Jenny laughing, running, her braid flying like the tail of a spirited filly. I had her undo her hair, let it fall. Circled her sitting there. I had her gently raise skeins of it against the low red light of the late sun, took pictures backlighted, framing her face.

Through all this Jenny worked seriously with me. Sometimes lowered eyelids, sometimes a half-smile. She was patient, would turn a bit to get a shadow line exactly right. At the end I said, "You are really a very good model."

"I knew you were going to say that," said the untrammeled one.

Not satisfied with my work and my Nikon, I had them hold off long enough to go to the modest studio of an old friend, Wayne Baker. Wayne had done covers, commercial work, for me. Silent, almost a shy man, a third-generation portrait maker with his grandfather's unwieldy old wood-bodied camera. The Baker stuff was masterful. I asked him to take Diane and Jenny together so that we would have one for generations yet unborn of Diane in her soft beauty and Jenny at the threshold. Jenny with her flame of hair down. The old bellows camera captured them, soft light gleaming on Diane's long hair, as I will remember them forever.

I was invited to come along to the beauty parlor for the cutting. I declined the offer. No one pressed me.

Diane said the beauty shop grew quiet. Cindy Leslie carefully separated the braid from Jenny and handed it to her mother. There was not a dry eye in the house.

Then Cindy's gifted hands began to shape Jenny's now shoulder-length hair. To everyone's surprise Jenny had naturally curly, wavy hair. We never knew it with her hair always pulled back. She will be one of those rare women who can shampoo, rinse, dry, then shake their hair back into place looking as though they just came from the beauty parlor. How lucky can one get?

The second surprise was how different, how grown-up and beautiful, Jenny looked with her face framed in soft curls. She rushed into the house to show me, she knew in an instant how much I liked it. The braid was gone. Goodbye. Now the real Jenny.

Next day after school I asked her how it went.

"Two boys said I was ugly. One asked me to marry him." No report on what the females had to say.

Then another rash of picture taking, Jenny with her short hair. Plenty of extra prints made, lots of letters sent out to the family. And lastly, we did find one of those flat boxes, and Jenny's braid was placed there carefully, lovingly, and dated. Now only a bit of her past.

Jenny instantly became adept at managing her own hair and proud of it, too. The time for Camp Niwana was upon us. In the reception room deep in the east-Texas woods Jenny was all rushing and flocking with fellow Bluebirds. Diane and I stood aside, getting teary-eyed. This would be our longest separation, ten days.

We took her things over to the screen-walled hut she would live in, met her counselor, a teenaged girl. No TV, no air-conditioning; Jenny balked at making up her own cot. Her mother helped this one time, explaining that this was the way of things at camp.

With tension rising between them they finished the cot, and I walked up jauntily and bounced a quarter off the coverlet, telling them this was how we did it in the Army.

In the stony silence, I picked up my quarter and pocketed it. I stayed out of things after that.

On the fifty-mile trip home through the beautiful east-

Texas pines Diane explained the cot scene: Jenny's gambit to hold back the flood of her real feelings about the separation.

There was no phone at Camp Niwana, but the mail service was fast. Before the weekend when we had to decide whether to bring her home or leave her there we got a tragic letter from Jenny saying how homesick she was, "... but I only cry at night." Diane was ready to bring her home.

We drove to camp on the weekend. Walked to the main council lodge, where we could hear all the campers singing. Jenny spotted us, gave only a casual wave of the hand.

At the break we got arm's-length hugs from a tanned and brawny child who tossed off a casual "Oh, thanks for coming up, but I'm staying."

Diane looked crestfallen.

Next on the parents' day program the kids had an hour's free swim. Jenny strode along ahead of us, but kept looking back. I thought I could see little cracks and chinks starting to appear in her supercool armor.

A good swimmer, Jenny was smoother now. Some of the teenaged counselors who worked with her came up and told us what a pleasure she was to be with. Just as we were leaving the pool in the forest a youth skidded around the corner, stopped, looked square at Diane, said, "You must be Jenny's mother. She looks exactly like you."

Diane turned to me with a look of pure and utter triumph.

Back at the car, with departure at hand, Jenny suddenly began to crumble. "I'm just not sure," she whispered desperately.

We went over to the camp commissary and bought a little teddy bear she had wanted, so that she could have something to cuddle and sleep with. Diane was telling her of the seriousness of completing a task once begun. Jenny wavered. Her lip was wavering, too.

Then I told her that if she stayed I would buy seven surprise gifts, one for each day she stayed at camp, and she could open them on her first seven days back home.

Jenny's eyes gleamed. "Really? Seven surprises? I'll stay."
We didn't linger much after that.

An afternoon thunderstorm was brewing up. All the kids
were herded inside and we drove home in rain and lightning,
I feeling absolutely rotten about having bribed my daughter.

Her next letter said, "It thundered and lightning the night
you left and I was scared and homesick and cried a lot and fell
out of bed." There was more writing, but hard to read. Diane
and I felt terrible, we couldn't look at each other.

At the joyous reunion a week later, Jenny told us as she
packed to go and made fond farewells that she had not actually fallen out of bed. "I just had some space left on the
page and put that in there to fill it up," she said blithely.

Then the little freckle face grinned up at me, exactly the
way I can remember grinning at my parents when I knew I
had them.

The seven surprises were a big success. Jenny opened one
each morning of the first week she was home. She had earned
her surprises, had seen it through the first time she needed to,
and there was some indefinable sureness about her that we
had not seen before.

She told us camp stories, and finally let us know that she
would like to go back for the last week of camp if she could.
So Jenny went back for another week.

We had pushed our little bird out of the nest, and she flew.

CHAPTER 32

She Never Looked Back

It was summertime, 1984. Jenny would soon be seven years old. I lay abed reading. Jenny came softly into my room, checking to see if I was awake and, if so, good for any games. She stood beside the bed, eyes dancing, full of some new idea, some scheme; I would know soon enough.

I looked up at her. "Hi, daughter. I sure do like you."

"I like you, too," she said and sat at the edge of the bed. I tousled her thick wavy hair; she smiled and said, "Dad, what's it like to see the sunrise?"

"Beautiful. Best time of day. The whole world is quiet and still. Fools are not up yet. There are never any two sunrises alike. There are sunrises of gold and purple splendor beneath the clouds. There are clear and brilliant sunrises, and on a dark and cloudy day no sunrise at all.

"What's it like on a cloudy day?"

"You just become aware that the night is passing. Things get easier to see, lighter shades of gray. Why do you ask?"

"Oh, just giving you some material for the book."

The book, I decided, was over. I had been waiting for some kind of a sign, anyway.

Did I miss anything in the telling? How about the time when she was five and came in, all serious and sober, sat beside me and asked me to tell her the most important thing she'd need to know for when she was grown up. I said, "Come back in ten minutes."

Ten minutes of serious thought and soul searching. She was back, and I was satisfied I had found a worthy answer for her.

"Two things, daughter, both easy to remember. The first is from the Bible. It is so short, so simple, that we have come to call it the Golden Rule. Here is it: 'Do unto others as you would have them do unto you.'

"The second is from Shakespeare, who was a great English writer. He lived a long time ago, but many of the things he wrote are as true today as they were then. In a play called *Hamlet*, Shakespeare wrote, 'This above all, to thine own self be true.' "

Jenny was silent a moment, nodded sagely, then she was gone. Off to something else.

"How'd I do?" I asked Diane, who had been listening from her end of the couch. She made no comment. I went on. "What a remarkable person we are sending into the twenty-first century. What happened to women like her in the Victorian age, and even before that?" Sure bait for Diane, I knew.

She was quick to reply. "They were taught out of the Bible and by every other means to be submissive. That men were superior to women."

"What a waste of humanity," I said.

"Do you realize how far you have come in your thinking?" asked Diane. Then, with a little grin and in exactly the same tone of voice she uses to talk to that half-witted tomcat Keats, she said, "Come here, and I'll give you a pat on the head."

I had started for her when the phone rang.

"I'll get it," called Jenny. Then, "It's Joyce. Can I go over to her house and play?"

"I'll walk you to the corner," I called back. That was our agreement. Joyce lived less than two blocks away, her house in view from the corner across a through street.

"Don't cross the street with me, Dad. Let me go on alone from here."

I stood and watched her look both ways, then run to her

little friend's house. Through sun and shadow, light glinting
in her hair. So strong. So eager.

She never looked back. She doesn't need to look back anymore. I don't know why I felt that so sharply. Daddies raise
daughters only to give them away. But I dread my growing
old and dying, and I am so flawed and time is running out so
fast. With Jenny I can go in peace. For I would rather leave
Jenny on this earth than the Pyramids.

About the Author

Best known as an aviation writer, "Bax" has been a feature columnist for *Flying* magazine since 1970. His two aviation books, *Bax Seat* and *How to Fly*, won national awards for aviation non-fiction. *How to Fly* is still in print (Summit Books) and *Bax Seat* is available from the author at his home in Beaumont, Texas.

Baxter writes for *Car & Driver*, a feature column since 1980, and recently began a column in *The Yacht*. He is going into his fortieth year of morning radio in Beaumont and twenty-fifth year of self-syndicated newspaper columns "that never got out of Texas." You can hear him weekly on National Public Radio's "All Things Considered," a veteran of five years with NPR.

"I am a stringer for the magazines, do freelance radio and TV, used to wonder what I was—writer or broadcaster. Decided I am a teller of tales, and the mike, camera, or pen is only incidental."

A pre-Jenny book, the story of Bax and Diane, called *Village Creek*, was published by Summit Books. A paperback is now available from Shearer Publishing, Bryan, Texas.

In younger days Bax reported from the eye of nine Gulf-coast hurricanes, from America's revolution of the sixties at Selma and Oxford, and was a combat correspondent during the '68 Tet Offensive in Vietnam.